Catholic Colleges in the 21st Century

A Road Map for Campus Ministry

JEFFREY LABELLE, SJ, AND
DANIEL KENDALL, SJ

Paulist Press
New York/Mahwah, NJ

Cover design by Sharyn Banks
Book design by Lynn Else

Library of Congress Cataloging-in-Publication Data

LaBelle, Jeffrey.
    Catholic colleges in the 21st century : a road map for campus ministry / Jeffrey LaBelle and Daniel Kendall.
        p. cm.
    Includes bibliographical references.
    ISBN 978-0-8091-4733-5 (alk. paper)
    1. Church work with students—Catholic Church. 2. Catholic universities and colleges—United States. 3. Church work with students—United States. I. Kendall, Daniel. II. Title.
    BX2347.8.S8L33 2011
    259′.24088282—dc22

                                                                        2011008863

Published by Paulist Press
997 Macarthur Boulevard
Mahwah, New Jersey 07430

www.paulistpress.com

CONTENTS

PREFACE

IN NOVEMBER OF 2008, the editors of Paulist Press approached us with an idea for a book on young Catholics in the postmodern context. With their encouragement and guidance, we have produced this current study to respond more specifically to the changing social, moral, and spiritual context of students on American Catholic college and university campuses. After extensive consultation with our editor and numerous professionals in campus ministry and student affairs across the country, we developed the scope of this work to include those issues and concerns reflected in the broad variety of campuses in the United States that are sponsored by Catholic dioceses and religious congregations. We are particularly indebted to our immediate editor, Chris Bellitto, for his keen direction in helping us frame the content contained here, as well as to the particular audience that we address: namely, current and future campus ministers on Catholic college campuses in the twenty-first century.

Prior to writing this volume, we had extensive phone conferences with Tim Muldoon of Boston College, the author of *Seeds of Hope: Young Adults and the Catholic Church in the United States*. In his book, Muldoon investigated the current social context of young adult Catholics concerning the practice of their faith. Our phone conferences with Tim led us to narrow the scope of the present work to focus on campus ministry and how it approaches the spiritual, social, and moral needs of students on Catholic college campuses in the United States.

Throughout this process, we learned that student life and religious expression have changed dramatically since the 1960s and '70s, the era of the Second Vatican Council. Young adults currently leaving high school and enrolling in Catholic colleges and universities experience life and faith in ways unique from their parents and grandparents, who were participants in the changes in the Church during those Vatican II decades. In fact, today many young college students find their social and academic lives rather disjointed from their spiritual or faith lives. This book is an attempt to address some of the challenges generated by this disconnect and to guide campus ministers toward more effective methods of serving the spiritual, social, and moral needs of the twenty-first-century college student.

The chapters of this book are organized by themes generated from phone and face-to-face conversations with a wide range of student affairs and campus ministry professionals. Within each thematic area, a number of issues arose during our chats that have helped us respond to a series of core questions developed across the weeks and months of our research. By way of introduction, let us take a quick glance at each theme and the primary questions that we address in each:

Chapter 1 deals with *Catholic college identity* and all that goes along with that concerning mission and core values. How can campus ministry play a role in the mission and identity of a Catholic college or university?

Chapter 2 develops *a profile of the students on Catholic college campuses* today. What are the demographics of these students from a social, cultural, and religious perspective?

Chapter 3 looks at *the role of the campus minister* and how that role can respond to the changing student culture on Catholic college campuses. What formal training do campus ministers need, and how does their role fit in with the rest of what happens on campus?

Chapter 4 delves into the issue of *the integration of academic life and campus ministry*. How does campus ministry relate to and interface with student academic life, and with theology and religious studies faculty?

Chapter 5 scopes out the *position of campus ministry among the plethora of college activities* that vie for college students' out-of-class time. How does campus ministry relate to and collaborate with service learning, volunteerism, and immersion programs?

Chapter 6 investigates the ways in which *campus ministry plays a role in student life in general.* How does campus ministry serve college students in regard to their social, moral, and spiritual development, especially their interpersonal relationships?

Chapter 7 reviews the integration of campus ministry into Catholic colleges' efforts to *promote social and political engagement* among its students. How can campus ministry encourage students to appropriate a faith that does justice?

Finally, based upon our discussion of the current context of young adults on Catholic college campuses, chapter 8 puts forth a vision of *the emergent Church of the twenty-first century as a response to the pastoral, spiritual, and social needs of today's emerging adults.*

In addition, at the end of each chapter, we provide a list of recommended books, articles, and other resources to assist in the ongoing professional development of campus ministers.

Some fascinating, overarching issues arose during our conversations with professionals on Catholic college campuses. For example, from a student affairs perspective, we learned of the development by the Association for Student Affairs at Catholic Colleges and Universities (ASACCU) of *Principles for Good Practice for Student Affairs at Catholic Colleges and Universities* (2007). These eight principles can serve as mileposts to gauge outcomes and progress in student affairs work, as well as to shed some light on the relationship that student affairs professionals perceive they have with campus ministry at U.S. Catholic colleges and universities. We refer to these principles throughout the book as they relate to the various themes under discussion.

On a thematic note, sexuality and sexual morality surfaced as areas of great concern and interest. These topics, in combination with spirituality, are treated rather extensively in Donna Freitas's recent (2008) *Sex and the Soul.* In her research, Freitas interviewed college students at a wide variety of private, public, and religious campuses across the country. Her findings shed light on the attitudes, perceptions, and lived morality of college students in the twenty-first century. Further, her conclusions point to some of the same concerns that surfaced in conversations with campus ministers: most especially noteworthy of these is the disconnect between sexual behavior and spirituality among American college students. This thematic arena provides a rich focus and challenge for campus ministry today.

We wish to express our gratitude to so many who have helped us along the way to bring this project to fruition. From the very beginning of our initial proposal, Chris Bellitto nudged and encouraged us to seek out advice and consultation to frame the scope of this book to better serve campus ministers. Tim Muldoon was instrumental in giving us the feedback we needed to realize the value of pursuing the themes we have taken up in this volume. Numerous campus ministers, student affairs personnel, administrators, and friends from across the country contributed their perspectives and gave their advice as well as their critique of our proposal and our choice of thematic content. These include Doug Leonhardt, Andy Thon, Ed Matthie, Margaret Higgins, Donal Godfrey, Jack Treacy, Mario Prietto, Jim Erps, Frank Majka, Mike Moynahan, Patrick Dorsey, and many others. We are extremely grateful to all who have played a part in this effort.

Jeffrey LaBelle, SJ, and Daniel Kendall, SJ
July 31, 2010

CHAPTER ONE

CAMPUS MINISTRY ON CATHOLIC COLLEGE CAMPUSES

THE SECOND VATICAN COUNCIL (1962–65) provides a good place to begin a study of campus ministry. The Council itself recognized the "social and cultural transformation" that was taking place in the world, changes that had repercussions on people's social and religious lives.[1] Before the Council, the term *campus ministry* was not a common part of the vocabulary at Catholic colleges and universities. Instead, people on the Catholic college scene would speak about the college "chaplain," discuss specific religious organizations such as the Sodality or Knights of Columbus, argue about the many academic requirements in philosophy and theology, question the value of having a mandatory retreat at the beginning of the academic year, and, frequently enough, wonder about the roles of the priests and sisters who taught in the various institutions. Usually most members of the student body were Catholics who had attended a Catholic secondary school. Both they and their parents were happy with the "safe" atmosphere provided by a Catholic institution of higher education. These same students have since become parents. When they accompany their sons and daughters who are seniors in high school to visit various Catholic college campuses, which usually include their own alma mater, they find a different atmosphere. The changes they witness often make them wonder about the "Catholicity" of these institutions. What has happened in the last half-century to make alumni even ask such a question? Let us look at some of the factors involved.

In 1967, two years after the Vatican Council ended, Father Theodore Hesburgh, CSC, president of Notre Dame University and president of the International Federation of Catholic Universities, convoked a seminar of Catholic educators at Land O' Lakes, Wisconsin. At the end of the meetings, the twenty-six participants signed a document that reflected their views. Among those who attended the meeting were university presidents, lay trustees, and religious superiors. The three bishops present (who all supported the final document) were Bishop John Dougherty (chairman of the Episcopal Committee for Catholic Higher Education), Archbishop Paul Hallinan from Atlanta, and Cardinal Theodore McCarrick, who was then president of the Catholic University of Puerto Rico.

According to the "Statement on the Nature of the Contemporary Catholic University," institutions of higher learning should possess the following characteristics: (1) be a university in the full sense of the word, with a strong commitment to and concern for academic excellence; (2) be a community of learners that has a social existence and an organizational form; and (3) reflect the Christian spirit and find profound and creative ways for the service of society and the people of God. The document encouraged inner-city social action, personal aid to the educationally disadvantaged, and exploration of new forms of Christian living, of Christian witness, and of Christian service. One's Christianity should be expressed in a variety of ways and be lived experientially and experimentally.

Theological disciplines, they maintained, are essential to the integrity of a Catholic university. Thus, the theology faculty members need to be in contact with other areas of study, and to dialogue with them, especially through interdisciplinary studies. This involves research as well as actively serving the Church and society.

To do all this, the Catholic university must have true autonomy and academic freedom—essential conditions of its life, growth, and survival.[2] This final point has caused many conservative Catholics to say that those who subscribe to this statement have rejected the teaching authority of the Catholic Church.

To face the changing composition of the student body and the globalization of the world, most of these institutions of higher education consider campus ministry the key to communicating and maintaining the Catholic identity of their institutions. Some Catholic colleges and universities have an office of mission and vision (or mission and identity).[3] Where no office of mission and vision exists, the institution relies even more heavily on campus ministry.

The principal role of campus ministry can best be described as that of a Catholic presence, which may be expressed by members of the team who are working in the residence halls, conducting liturgies, leading or helping with retreats, attending various campus events, giving theological reflections at immersion experiences, initiating faculty discussion groups, or showing students how to use their talents to serve others. Just as Vatican II was "pastoral" in its documents (a synonym for *practical*), so campus ministry's task is to make Christ's presence known in the daily lives of college students (as well as of their teachers, staff, and administrators) in the twenty-first century. This emphasis on the centrality of Christ has always been the mark of a Catholic institution; campus ministry strives to make it practical at all levels.

A look at the demographics of many Catholic institutions of higher education highlights some challenges that face a campus ministry team. Unlike the role of the college chaplain, who frequently concentrated on the spiritual welfare of undergraduate students, campus ministry also currently concerns itself with faculty, administrators, staff, and graduate students, as well as the traditional undergraduates. Its focus is much broader than the previous model. In addition, an increasing number of non-Catholic students enroll at Catholic universities more than ever. These students (as well as faculty members) come from diverse ethnic and religious backgrounds.[4] Both they and their Catholic counterparts have been affected by the increasing secularization of

3

today's world; frequently enough, both groups know very little about the faith that they each profess (if they even have a religious affiliation at all).[5] Sometimes a hostile attitude is present ("I came here for an education, not all this religious stuff"). Anecdotally, a few faculty or staff members will sometimes candidly admit that they are more interested in the convenience of the institution's location and the salary they receive than in the "religious atmosphere" of the college or university. Campus ministry teams need to address this modern reality. Just where should a response begin and what should it be?

Institutions of higher education have developed rather detailed mission statements. Over time, these documents are revised in light of changing historical, sociological, and economic circumstances, among other factors. Yet continuity with the past influences the present reality. Thus, graduates of Catholic institutions should expect certain core values to remain part of their mission. Likewise, when faculty or staff members are hired and when students are accepted into programs, they become part of an institution that has a particular set of explicit values and goals. A Catholic college or university has a connection to a specific faith and is not just a secular enterprise. Hence, persons who become part of the institution must be open to its Catholic identity, even if they are not Catholics themselves. Most realize that the Catholic identity will be reflected in both the academic programs, as well as in the overall atmosphere of the institution.

Although a Catholic college or university has a connection to an explicit faith, it nevertheless needs to be welcoming and inclusive of others who do not share that faith. It has an obligation to provide for the diversity of the people it serves.[6] This means engaging people both formally and informally: a college meets people where they are. This is accomplished by interacting with them on both a one-to-one basis as well as something more formal. Campus ministry helps make explicit what is implicit in the mission statement in a way that respects people's diverse backgrounds. Doing this is a challenge because the world is constantly evolving and changing.

Campus Ministry on Catholic College Campuses

Because of the diversity of the people whom colleges and universities serve, campus ministry programs vary widely. Yet some issues are common to all colleges. The recent world economic crisis has shown just how materialistic are the values that some people embrace. The media frequently reinforce these consumerist values.[7] One result is that today many people are rethinking what is important in their lives. On the other hand, the values of some people who say that they are Catholics are often the same as those who call themselves secular humanists. Both want a better world. In such a context the task of campus ministry is that of leading people to understand how witnessing to the Gospel is a liberating and socially responsible message. How can this best be accomplished?

A traditional way that campus ministry deals with Catholics is to provide religious services that are geared to a college environment. The most obvious inroad is having liturgies where the choice of presiders, selection of music, and preparation of homilies are geared not only for students, but also have the faculty and staff in mind. This approach also implies that the campus ministry team has a keen awareness of current college culture and contemporary issues. In addition to events that are strictly liturgical, campus ministry usually sponsors Kairos retreats, Cursillo, and CYO Search Retreats. These are especially effective with undergraduates because they involve students working with students. Older "authority" figures remain in the background and serve as resource persons. Non-Catholics are welcome to participate in both the religious services and retreats, and often present thought-provoking viewpoints. Frequently enough, long-established Catholic culture plays a minor role with some contemporary Catholics because they have very little religious history. Other "traditional" Catholic approaches involve exposure to the other sacraments (beyond the celebration of the Eucharist) and to practices such as the Stations of the Cross, Las Posadas, and so on. Involving both Catholics and non-Catholics enriches lecture series and, most especially, discussion groups. This is quite evident in Bible study groups, sacramental preparation, and even "courses" in preparing people to be received into the Church through the Rite of Christian Initiation of Adults (RCIA).

At most Catholic colleges and universities, campus ministry also reaches out to non-Catholics. Though their numbers on campus may vary, they are part of the college community; so their inclusion and collaboration are necessary if they are to participate fully in the mission of the institution. Thus, campus ministry encourages these students to join clubs, such organizations as InterVarsity Christian Fellowship, and so on. Naturally, the campus ministry offices usually provide a list of nearby places of worship. In some of the larger institutions, a rabbi or Protestant minister might have a position on the campus ministry team; and the college or university might furnish a suitable place for the Muslim students to worship. In any event, campus ministry should most certainly act as a liaison for assisting diverse populations to find God in their lives.

Most institutions of higher education sponsor "immersion programs." This particular approach to combining learning and experience has been around a long time. Modern language departments in colleges have long supported curricula in which students live abroad in a foreign country for a certain amount of time. In a similar effort to raise people's awareness of their neighbors as well as to make their faith more practical, campus ministry teams in various institutions have encouraged and organized similar experiences over the years. They have become so popular that other college departments have adopted this method. In some institutions not only the students but the senior administrators are required to take part in an immersion experience. Sometimes an immersion experience is part of a graduation requirement.

In itself, an immersion program is not necessarily religious. Its main purpose is to facilitate learning by people living in a particular environment. If a person travels to a foreign country and lives with a family that speaks a foreign language, the results can usually be measured. At the end of the experience, others can judge how well that person can speak the "new" language. Thus, certain expectations are built into the structure of the program. Whether or not these expectations have been met can be determined by some type of test or evaluation at the end of the experience.

In contrast, we cannot measure the effectiveness of a religious immersion experience so easily. What test can be given? Of course, any immersion experience can be so structured that certain results can be anticipated. For instance, when campus ministry offers a certain experience, it obviously expects some results. These results should have some reference to the religious life of the participants. On a very practical level of organization, that means deciding the size of the group, telling the group why this particular format was chosen, preparing the group to keep the goals in mind, reflecting with the group as the experience continues, and then evaluating the experience after the immersion has concluded. Let us look at an example to help clarify this.

Gonzaga University's School of Engineering received a grant to conduct a program entitled "Engineering beyond Borders." Its purpose was to provide people in developing countries (in this case, a country in Africa) with clean water. Some people might say that such a goal is noble in itself and really does not need the involvement of campus ministry. Students learn much from such an experience. In this particular case, however, in addition to the technical knowledge that the students were to learn, they were also prepared by campus ministry to consider the connections between faith and good works. Good works are an expression of one's faith. During the two-week trip someone from campus ministry who had accompanied the group helped students to reflect each day on their many new experiences. Students were also asked to keep a diary. After they had returned home, they were given guidelines on how to write up their notes and reflect on their experiences. They earned academic credit while learning about both engineering and religion. Though this particular experience was conducted with a Catholic viewpoint in mind, it cut across religious boundaries.

In a fairly recent document, Muslim leaders sent a letter to the pope in which they affirmed their desire to build peaceful and friendly relationships based on the shared Abrahamic tradition of love of God and love of neighbor.[8] Their same position was repeated in a subsequent document, "A Common Word between Us and You,"[9] which stressed the mutual love of God for all people, and challenged Christians to establish relationships with their Muslim neighbors based on love.[10] Likewise, most other religions advocate a similar position. The two-week immersion experience in Africa brought together many different perspectives: experiencing love of neighbor and one's obligations toward that neighbor, learning something about engineering in a Third World country, and reflecting in an organized way on how "love of neighbor" should be a concrete part of daily life.

What would this immersion experience have been like without the input of campus ministry? Most likely, the students would have gained a lot of experience just from the trip itself. They would have realized how poor other people are, and how much assistance they need. No doubt a faculty or staff leader would have asked the students to consider some moral and ethical perspectives of their situation. The immersion trip would probably have been very profitable, and, when recalled years later, those who were involved would most likely say that it was one of the highlights of their lives. On the other hand, if there had been no guidance from campus ministry, people might reasonably have asked, "What was so Catholic or religious about the trip? What part of it was faith based? Were the leaders able to make the connection between the students' experiences and faith?" Following up on that, others might question the (religious) backgrounds of both the students and leaders: "Did they come from a secular mentality? Were those the values that the leaders were passing on? How qualified were the leaders in imparting a 'Catholic' viewpoint? Were they even interested in doing so? Since the word *Catholic* appeared in the institution's mission statement, how were its core values reflected in such a program?" An immersion program such as the one just described provides a valuable opportunity for a Catholic institution to implement and promote its mission. Though the trip and experience had been organized by the school of engineering, campus ministry was able to provide a religious presence, and challenged people to reframe their experiences in a wider context. It made the immersion truly *catholic* in the widest sense of the word.

Assessment is the operative word in higher education today. Not only do colleges and universities frequently evaluate the teachers and students, but they look at the effectiveness of the programs themselves:[11] how is the money being spent, and what are the results? Let's take an example to show the need for assessment. As part of his recent doctoral dissertation (2010), John Savard undertook a survey of the effectiveness of international immersion programs in seventeen Jesuit colleges and universities. How did these programs impact the religiosity of the students who participated? These programs took place during the breaks in the academic year 2008 to 2009. The countries involved were located in North and South America, Central America, as well as island countries such as Jamaica and the Dominican Republic. Amazingly the total number of students combined from all seventeen universities was only about 450.[12] Given these enrollment figures, the institutions themselves need to evaluate all such programs to ascertain whether or not they are effectively imparting the mission and values of each institution, especially with the high costs involved. A second consideration is why a college or university should sponsor such programs if only relatively few students are served while the vast majority are not. This example can be applied to other programs, especially those with which campus ministry is involved.

Each organization has its own structures. These structures change as needs vary and new priorities develop. Each college or university determines where campus ministry fits into its hierarchy of administration. Although countless factors go into deciding the role of its director and staff, both the values of the institution and the available funding are elements that are involved in any discussion. A structure shows, at least partially, the importance (or lack thereof) that an office or program has in carrying out the mission and vision of the institution.

Catholic Colleges in the 21st Century

Let us consider three structural models for campus ministry. In some institutions, campus ministry reports directly to the president. At a quick glance, this first structural arrangement indicates that campus ministry has a special place in the institution. The president, along with the trustees or directors, sets the policies. Obviously what the president considers a value will usually be given priority by the other collaborators. The views of the director of campus ministry will certainly be considered in policy decisions. The negative side of such an arrangement is that people frequently consider campus ministry as simply an appendage of the president's office, and not as an important entity in itself. It lacks a certain freedom, such as providing a diverse but necessary voice in the community. For all practical purposes, in this arrangement directors of campus ministry become major administrators who spend much time attending meetings with other administrators, and who often become distant from the people whom they serve: the students and faculty, and even their own staffs.

In another structural model, campus ministry becomes a "department" under a vice president for student life. Since both campus ministry and student life play major roles in the mission and identity of the institution, they are not just referral sources. They complement each other, and each usually runs immersion and service programs. Both have undergraduate students as their primary focus, though campus ministry most often also includes faculty, graduate students, and, sometimes, alumni. Yet we need to consider the differences in the two departments and the problems that arise because of these differences.

Today's world tends to be secular; people often accept Catholic values only grudgingly. Even in the setting of a Catholic college, students sometimes are secular themselves and not even culturally Catholic. Though those who oversee immersion and service programs often enough have the faith themselves, many do not know how to help students make connections between experience and faith. As a result, in this all-too-common situation, the tendency is to sponsor programs that are not faith based. Fulfilling graduation requirements rather than searching for a deeper faith is what most frequently occupies students. For instance, business students realize that they must experience an immersion or service program as part of their business major or minor; those whose major is in the field of arts and sciences know that in order to graduate they must work in a soup kitchen or a homeless shelter for a specified number of hours during their college years to experience cultural diversity or to be aware of the need for social justice. Most of today's students expect such requirements because colleges and universities are educating people to face the world around them, and try to provide relevant learning opportunities. Historically, programs such as these started in campus ministry but then were handed off later to other offices such as student affairs. The result is that the religious element is frequently bypassed.

Campus ministry provides the lens of faith through which people can view these programs. Practically speaking, the campus ministry team should somehow be involved with most of these programs. Such involvement entails being a presence at the level of preparation, offering reflections during the experience itself, and leading follow-up sessions with those who have been involved. The experience of those who have had an immersion trip needs to be brought to the awareness of the community at large. This does not happen easily if the campus ministry department is subordinate to the student life office. Ideally campus ministry should in some way be involved in the majority of immersion and service programs at a Catholic college or university.[13]

A third structural model to consider is when the offices of both campus ministry and student affairs are separate offices that report to the same person, probably at the vice presidential level. Though no model is perfect, this one probably has fewer negative components than the others just mentioned. This particular model highlights two areas that are concerned with the institution's mission and identity. Since each has a role to play, they sometimes overlap; however, they are usually complementary.

Both of these offices are vital to the mission and identity of the institution. Depending on the diversity of people in the institution, administrators generally try to recruit staffs that balance the many concerns of various people: ethnicity, religious preferences, sexual identity, gender issues (to name just a few). In a sense, members of both student life and campus ministry teams need to be ecumenical. Persons hired for a specific job need to be aware of other concerns. For instance: Who should decide when a person should be referred to the counseling center or a pastoral minister? Is a group that is applying for recognized "club" status really a dangerous "cult"? Who should deal with a student seriously injured in an automobile accident, and with that person's family? When a member of the community is charged with a crime, which office makes the official response? Solid reasons could be given for assuming that something "is a student life problem," or that "campus ministry should take care of it." Yet such areas are common to both campus ministry and student life, and fall within the purview of a single vice president. With the complexity of students' lives and the issues that people face, concerns like those just mentioned underscore the need for a strong and close relationship between campus ministry and student life offices.

Does the institution provide a menu of program options for students? "One size fits all" is not a credible approach. In sponsoring programs, campus ministry focuses on reflection, faith, and evaluation. In drawing up approaches, campus ministry needs to look at the demographics of the institution, especially with regard to the various faith traditions represented. In so doing, campus ministry does not act alone, but in conjunction with other departments of the institution. Keeping this in mind is important because this is where turf wars frequently develop, and where people are working at cross-purposes rather than with each other. As mentioned above, we live in an outcomes-assessment culture, so campus ministry needs to have specific goals and ways of assessing them.

For the campus ministry team to keep abreast of changes, its director needs to have frequent and regular meetings with the president.

The interchange of information and ideas is beneficial to both. The president needs an honest appraisal of how well programs are working, and what their good and bad aspects are. In order to understand the larger picture, the director must have input from the president about planned initiatives and the direction in which the institution is headed. Likewise, the directors of campus ministry should be invited to participate on a regular basis in meetings with people in related fields (like those in student life, those who represent various student organizations, and those who are discussion group leaders) to give input and receive information on the ways in which campus ministry can better serve the community.

All of these proposals that we have mentioned cost money; institutions do not have unlimited budgets. How then should campus ministry be funded since so much competition exists for limited financial resources? Like most institutions, colleges and universities have a board of trustees, in addition to the president, which decides the priorities. Members of the board usually come from different backgrounds, so they are able to bring a diversity of experience and judgment to the governance of an institution. Most members of the board have agreed to serve in that capacity because they believe in the mission and vision of the institution. For an institution that prides itself on being Catholic, that aspect should receive much attention. The question then is how best to support the mission and vision with the allocation of funds. A perennial observation has been that if campus ministry is so essential to the mission of the university, why is it frequently so poorly funded, especially with regard to the salaries of the team? Campus ministry in colleges and universities needs a dedicated budget line if it is to promote the values that the institution espouses. Many people would say that this is only logical, but in some schools, campus ministry depends on the largesse of the president during a particular year, and whatever money it can generate on its own. The institution's financial support should match its rhetoric about being a Catholic institution.

Newspapers and magazines often use a pie chart to explain finances. A pie is pictured on a page and the size of its slices represents the percentage of money allotted to a particular item. Just how much of the college or university's financial pie is devoted to campus ministry? Although this image could oversimplify the issues at stake, it can serve as a good indication of what an institution considers to be important. For instance: Do the salaries of members of the campus ministry team reflect the importance of what people are doing, as well as their professional preparation? Are there enough people on the team? Does the budget provide for the professional development and professional updating for members of the team? Such questions provide a good reality check of whether the advertising matches the facts.

The purpose of this chapter has been to give a general outline of campus ministry as it exists on most Catholic college and university campuses at the beginning of the twenty-first century: Where have Catholic colleges and universities been? Where are they now? And where are they going? These questions frame any discussion of campus ministry. Obviously, this implies a consideration of the Catholic mission, vision, and core values: How is Catholic identity balanced with religious and cultural pluralism? What is the relationship between student life and campus ministry? How do finances and the organizational structure enter into the discussion? These are some of the key questions that we have posed, along with some tentative answers. In subsequent chapters, we will pose further queries and propose additional responses regarding the current context of campus ministry at Catholic colleges and universities.

RECOMMENDED READING

For a comprehensive report of data about 112,000 participants from 236 colleges and universities, see the Higher Education Research Institute's *The Spiritual Life of College Students* (Los Angeles: UCLA, 2004). This study was conducted over a period of years and focuses on the inner development of students; that is, their "sphere of values and beliefs, emotional maturity, spirituality, and self-understanding."

Campus Ministry on Catholic College Campuses

The same Higher Education Research Institute surveyed over 40,000 faculty members nationwide to determine what college instructors believe and how those beliefs impact their teaching. Details of their findings can be found in *Spirituality and the Professorate: A National Study of Faculty Beliefs, Attitudes, and Behaviors* (Los Angeles: UCLA, 2004–5).

People often wonder just what a typical core curriculum in a Catholic institution of higher education entails at the beginning of the second millennium. A simple Web search can reveal what a particular university or college requires. Notre Dame University provides one good example of a comprehensive core curriculum. This can be found at http://www.nd.edu/~corecrlm/.

Reference has been made to the Land O' Lakes meetings and the resulting "Statement on the Nature of the Contemporary Catholic University." The actual document can be found at http://archives.nd.edu/ episodes/visitors/lol/idea.htm. Two good commentaries on the whole process have been given by David O'Brien (http://www.cabrini.edu/Library/documents/MissionTaskForce/DavidOBrienreflectiononLandOLakes1998.pdf) and Neil McCluskey (http://www.realcatholictv.com/cia/05rebellion/17. pdf).

A contemporary (1990) Vatican document on Catholic higher education is *Ex Corde Ecclesiae* ("From the Heart of the Church"), found at http://www.vatican.va/holy_father/john_paul_ii/apost _constitutions/documents/hf_jp-ii_apc_15081990_ex-corde-ecclesiae_en.html.

A brief description and background of the Kairos Retreat is available at http://en.wikipedia.org/wiki/Kairos_%28retreat%29.

CHAPTER TWO

STUDENT PROFILE ON CATHOLIC COLLEGE CAMPUSES

IN THIS CHAPTER WE WILL examine the various social factors that influence and shape the profile of students on Catholic college campuses today. As we have seen in the previous chapter, each generation has historically approached life on college campuses quite differently. Furthermore, the ways in which Catholic colleges and universities define themselves as Catholic have changed dramatically with the advent of the Second Vatican Council and the years following that historic event. Let us now turn to the demographic reality of students at Catholic colleges in the twenty-first century. Just who are they? And how do they identify themselves in regard to religious affiliation, career interest, lifestyle preferences, and so forth?

In order to respond to these questions about the demographics of Catholic colleges and universities, we need to look at the actual numbers. Currently 188 colleges and universities are active members of the National Catholic College Admissions Association (National CCAA).[1] However, taken from a broader perspective, according to the Association of Catholic Colleges and Universities (ACCU) Web site, the total number of Catholic colleges and universities is greater and breaks down as follows:

- 201 Catholic colleges and universities
- 28 freestanding Catholic seminaries that offer degrees for lay students

Student Profile on Catholic College Campuses

- 9 Catholic universities and colleges with seminaries
- 7 single-purpose institutions, such as freestanding law schools, medical schools, and nursing programs[2]

In comparative terms, the ACCU indicates that these traditional undergraduate Catholic colleges and universities comprise 201 out of a total of 4,453 institutions of higher education in the United States.[3] This means that Catholic institutions represent less than 5 percent of the total American colleges and universities. Of the 4.6 million Catholic college students in the United States, an estimated 500,000 are enrolled in Catholic institutions.[4] These 201 Catholic colleges and universities are distributed across the United States, but are concentrated along the Atlantic and Pacific coasts, as well as in the Midwest, with the South and West being underserved locally. Church attendance among Catholic students is a self-reported statistic that is available through Georgetown University's Center for Applied Research in the Apostolate (CARA). According to a September 2004 CARA poll of Catholics, ages 18 to 30, 21 percent self-report attending Mass once or more per week. This figure compares dramatically with 52 percent attending Mass at least once a week among pre–Vatican II Catholics and Vatican II Catholics who are above 43 years old.[5] Of course, these figures do not take into account church attendance by members of other religious denominations, nor do they indicate participation in other religious activities beyond organized Catholic liturgies.

In general, Catholic colleges and universities are composed of a wide range of students from differing religious backgrounds and affiliations. Percentages of self-identified Catholics attending these Catholic colleges and universities may range from a low of 20 percent to a high of 80 percent. "Generally, around 60 percent of incoming freshmen at four-year Catholic colleges and universities self-identify as Catholic."[6] In spite of the variation that can exist in these percentages, the demographic profiles of the current, typical U.S. Catholic college or university stand in sharp contrast to profiles of the student populations of the

1950s and 1960s, which were predominately male and 80 to 100 percent Catholic. According to the National CCAA, Catholic colleges and universities are now incredibly diverse:

1. They come in all sizes, with enrollments of fewer than 1,000 students to more than 20,000.
2. They are located in large cities and small towns from coast to coast. They are located in 40 states, the District of Columbia, and Puerto Rico.
3. They include women's colleges; major universities with law, medical, and other professional schools; a historically black university; and seven that grant pontifical degrees.[7]

So, what are the religious preferences among all college students in the United States today? According to the 2004 survey results of UCLA's Higher Education Research Institute (HERI), 28 percent identify themselves as having a religious preference as Roman Catholic.[8] This group represents the single largest religious preference group among those surveyed. The next largest category was "none" with 17 percent of the students listed in this group. However, if one were to combine all Christian affiliations other than Catholic, *that* would be the single most preferred religious group. Still, Roman Catholic college students represent an important and significant portion of our current higher education culture to take into account, whether they study at Catholic colleges or not.

This survey was conducted in 2003 to 2004 by UCLA's HERI researchers to better understand the spiritual and religious perspectives of college students across the country. In the introduction to their report, they narrate, "Today's entering college students report high levels of spiritual interest and involvement. Four in five indicate 'having an interest in spirituality' and 'believing in the sacredness of life,' and nearly two-thirds say that 'my spirituality is a source of joy.'"[9] The HERI researchers went on later in their report to summarize the profile of today's college students in the following descriptive narrative.

> Students coming to campuses today are a diverse group ethnically, socio-economically, religiously, and politically. While they have high ambitions and aspirations for educational and occupational success, and college is the means by which they believe they can realize their goals, they are also actively dealing with existential questions. They are searching for deeper meaning in their lives, looking for ways to cultivate their inner selves, seeking to be compassionate and charitable, and determining what they think and feel about the many issues confronting their society and the global community.[10]

Not surprisingly, many beginning college students choose their majors and degree programs primarily based upon their career plans. In other words, they tend to link higher education with a moneymaking outcome. This career focus can challenge their overall learning experience, as well as the extent to which they integrate their faith life with their personal identity development. This would lead a person to inquire which careers are popular among college students today, since their choices of majors often reflect their values and spirituality. According to the *Princeton Review* of 2009, the top ten undergraduate majors preferred by graduating high school seniors were the following: (1) business administration and management; (2) psychology; (3) elementary education and teaching; (4) nursing—registered nurse training; (5) biology/biological sciences; (6) education; (7) English language and literature; (8) political science and government; (9) economics; and (10) marketing/marketing management.[11] As one can readily surmise, several of these majors are service oriented, underscoring the current cultural value and strong motivation among young adults and college students to participate in service to society and its transformation.

Catholic Colleges in the 21st Century

In preparing to write this book, we posed the following question to the college professionals we consulted: "What are some of the current concerns and interests of students on Catholic college campuses?" In the remainder of this chapter, we will touch upon various issues and factors of student experience on Catholic college campuses. Each of these in itself can and does have a profound impact on the way in which campus ministers carry out their mission to serve their constituents, bearing the Catholic identity of the college they represent. In addition, these various elements play into one another to sometimes obscure and complicate the reality of the student context. Let us take a careful look at both lifestyle change and college culture on today's Catholic college campuses.

Several issues enter into the picture regarding the lifestyle of college students in the twenty-first century. These include, but are not limited to, sexual morality, cohabitation, parental support, and the impact and use of technology. These various cultural factors interplay to produce a rather dramatic shift in the ways in which young adults on Catholic college campuses (or any campus, for that matter) relate with one another, as well as with the faculty members and staffs at their institutions of higher education. Let's begin by looking at sexual morality, in particular as reflected in the lives of students on U.S. Catholic college campuses.

Campus ministers and student affairs personnel point to the many questions that college students pose about morality and their faith: What does the Church allow in the area of sexual activity and behavior? How can a person determine if he or she is life-giving in a relationship? How does one put into place an activity- or behavior-centered approach to sexuality? How can college students nurture and maintain healthy relationships? What does the Church offer GLBT (gay/lesbian/bisexual/transgender) students? Because many college students have the perception that the Church has a negative view of sexuality, certainly more and better preaching about relationships is warranted and could help in this regard. But a much more effective and beneficial approach would include discussion groups among peers (without the presence of campus ministers), since students often feel a need for anonymity and privacy. Clearly none of these questions can be effectively answered in one or two sentences: a great deal of loving, patient dialogue is needed to guide young adults to discover how to live out their faith appropriately in the current cultural context.

Today's college students, not unlike previous generations, are open to living situations of different kinds, including coed or mixed residence halls and apartments. In the past, these housing opportunities were most often orchestrated to provide students with a social life that allowed for more fraternal or communitarian interaction. Buildings were designed in such a way as to ensure privacy, with separation of men and women by floors, sections, or suites. In the current context, many college students are not only open to coed or mixed living situations, but even welcome and prefer mixed gender roommates. Although some colleges and universities provide for these options, most often these are off-campus housing possibilities. At times, these arrangements are for financial reasons. At other times, they are based upon friendships prior to the college years or associations with alumni from the same high schools. In short, cohabitation is not uncommon among Catholic college students, but does not necessarily indicate partnering or sexual activity among friends. In the past, *cohabitation* usually was a term used exclusively for couples in a sexual relationship. With the coming of what's been labeled the "hook-up culture," these types of committed cohabitation arrangements are waning.

The current generation of college students has been described as more connected to parents and family members than previous generations. It is not uncommon for twenty-first-century college students to use their cell phones to check in with parents and siblings on a daily, if not hourly, basis for advice and support. This tendency stands in stark contrast to the sixties' and seventies' generations that were more socially distant from their parents by intention. Such constant communication would have been unthinkable in those days. In fact, one attrac-

21

tion of going away to college was just that: to get away from parental control. Perhaps with the shrinking size of the nuclear family and the technological advances in communication, later generations have developed a greater value in staying connected with home. In any event, college students now tend to seek out parental and familial support to an extent parallel with the generations during the first half of the twentieth century.

Many students struggle with their personal identity during their college years, which includes their religious identity. This is most often seen in the struggle to come to terms with the role that faith or religious tradition plays in their lives. Furthermore, college years are often opportunities for questions or doubts to surface about how young adults deal with their religious identity.

This leads us to the impact of technology on college students and, for that matter, people in general in the twenty-first century. Texting, instant messaging, phone calls, and e-mails have enabled young adults to have virtual and instantaneous contact with those they love. Anyone walking around a U.S. college campus today between classes can witness the plethora of young adults talking on cell phones as they make their way to their next session. It is not uncommon for groups of college friends to be walking together, yet each on a cell phone talking to different friends or family members. Face-to-face communication frequently gives way to virtual communication as the preferred mode of contact. This cultural shift has deeply affected the way in which college students relate to one another, to faculty members, and to those they love. Technology has altered the timing, means, and style of our social interaction dramatically. This is the context of the college student in the postmodern world.

It is quite clear that present-day college students prefer to use electronic media to communicate with family, friends, and instructors. The means include cell phones, text messaging, Twitter, and social communication networks. These latter methods are quite popular as sites to hook up with friends. Some examples are Myspace, Facebook, and other blog sites, which allow the posting of pictures, video clips, and other personal information to help people get acquainted in a quasi-anonymous, less-threatening fashion. Young adults find that these media allow them maximum freedom and spontaneity in their relationships. They use these techniques with great physical dexterity and emotional comfort.

Just how do campus ministers come to grips with this cultural shift in the twenty-first century? Certainly, all of these technological advances are useful tools to tap into in order to communicate with students. Campus ministers would do well to develop podcasts, streaming videos, social networking sites, and other media to reach out to college students in the most effective way to communicate with them. In short, the call and the challenge are to meet the students where they are. This means embracing a technologically savvy approach to communicating the word of God to reach more of the people of God on Catholic college campuses in the United States.

In addition to these changes in communication styles, socializing and building relationships have become even more complex in the postmodern world because they involve further considerations regarding contemporary dating habits. It is quite common among college students on both public and private campuses to get caught up in the hook-up culture of the twenty-first century. This entails an attitudinal and behavioral shift among young adults in which couples hook up for short-term relationships without intending any commitment or engagement. Outside the realm of dating, hooking up has as its goal sexual and emotional gratification without strings. In addition, it allows total freedom to experiment without making any promises. Clearly, this cultural value or quasi norm among college students presents a unique challenge to traditional Catholic values and mores.

According to Donna Freitas in her book *Sex and the Soul*: "Hooking up is part of a broader process of sexual experimentation, which in [one student's] view is part and parcel of the Catholic college experience."[12] This attitude stands in sharp contrast to the faith practice of evangelical Christians. "Unlike evangelical students," Freitas continues, "whose concerns about sex are inextricably connected to their religious tradition and spiritual identity, most students at the spiritual colleges keep sex and religion separate."[13] Here she refers to Catholics and others who, in name, espouse a particular sexual morality, but, in practice, live another. Freitas relates her rather surprising experience when encountering Catholic students:

> I have occasionally met young people who practice "Catholic orthodoxy" when it comes to sex, but I didn't interview a single college student who fit this description. The average Catholic student I interviewed was either clueless about Catholicism's teachings about sex or didn't care. Whatever Catholic sexual ethics these students have acquired, they acquired by osmosis.[14]

In general, many Catholic colleges and universities have made great strides in promoting their mission and identity as Catholic institutions. In part, this is an attempt to promote Catholic values among the students attending these institutions. The hope is that these values will foster and enhance self-identity and self-confidence in the lives of these young adults, values that are accented more in a school with a mission and identity. However, the question remains as to how these outcomes might be measured. Many Catholic institutions have developed measurements to begin this process via senior surveys and core curriculum assessments.[15]

At the beginning of the twenty-first century, college students were less involved in political activity than in previous generations. However, since 9/11, interest in politics has been growing in popularity among college students in general. In 2009, HERI reported, "A record number of incoming college students are politically engaged, with 85.9 percent reporting that they frequently or occasionally discussed politics in the last year [2008]."[16] In addition, today's college students have a growing social awareness. They seem to be highly motivated to participate in service projects, whether as part of a course's service-learning requirement or as an intentional immersion experience directed by campus ministry or other campus organizations. However, they often lack the tools and opportunities to reflect on these experiences from a faith perspective and to examine their motivations for participating in them. For example, many service opportunities are extremely popular, but campus ministers and other college personnel need to assist college students in making the connection between faith and justice. How do we help students reflect on their values, dispositions, motivations, and goals? Too often, the motivation of current college students to engage in service is limited to a secular humanist volunteerism, which can tend to be self-seeking and self-aggrandizing. "Today, the challenge is to reconnect religion and spirituality; what is interesting is that many young people are discovering for themselves that they need them both."[17]

College students, in general, have a much greater interest in spirituality rather than in institutionalized religion. In fact, this tendency plays into a trend toward avoiding commitment to one or another religion. Contributing further to this separation, their spirituality tends to be more individualistic than communal. Many Catholic college students perceive very little relevance of the Church's teaching in regard to their personal lives because of scandals, statements about sexuality, and other ethical issues. To put it quite simply, the students experience a disconnect between their sexual experience and their chosen spirituality or religion.

For many, the very term *religion* has, over the years, become synonymous with *restrictive*. Where religion is about following rules, spirituality is about creating a meaningful life; where religion is about obedience to authority, spirituality is about freedom of conscience; where religion is about dusty traditions and stifling rituals, spirituality is about living the truth creatively. These are unhappy caricatures, both of religion and of spirituality.[18]

All of this leads us to a consideration of personal and social values among college students. Just how do these young adults sort out their values, while faced with so many other conflicting ones from today's societal and peer pressures? Certainly they are challenged, as many people are in today's fast-paced American culture, to find time for prayer, reflection, and quiet. They are often caught up in a whirlwind of active participation in many fascinating pursuits. But without time, silence, and space to critically reflect upon their relationships and activities, they may lack the faith integration to help them sort out the meaning of their lives. As Muldoon offers, "We need to be held responsible for our prayer lives."[19] This is certainly true on Catholic college campuses across the United States nowadays.

After reporting the results of their 2004 survey, HERI concluded:

> Students choosing Roman Catholic as their religious preference tend to score below the overall average on four measures: Religious Commitment, Religious Engagement, Religious/Social Conservatism, and Religious Skepticism. The Catholics' relatively low score on Skepticism is unusual, in the sense that students with low scores on the first three measures of religiousness ordinarily earn *high* scores on Religious Skepticism (e.g., Jewish students, Unitarians, Buddhists, and "Nones").[20]

These findings point to a tension among Catholic college students: a peculiar disparity between their self-identified religious affiliation and their lived experience of that religion. Campus ministers must deal with this conflict between faith and practice in order to effectively carry out their mission to serve young Catholics on America's college campuses. The four measures cited in the HERI survey provide a clear focus for the attention of campus ministry in the twenty-first century: religious engagement, religious commitment, religious/social conservatism, and religious skepticism. These areas should be addressed openly and directly in the development of campus ministry programs and training. Finally, they find expression in the various hot-button issues mentioned by professionals across the country: sexual identification/orientation issues, service orientation, disconnectedness between Church and sexuality, overdependence on parental guidance, and relativism in the values and moral practice that are often divorced from one's personal spirituality.

RECOMMENDED READING

For a more thorough treatment of the concept of emerging adulthood, see Jeffrey Arnett's *Emerging Adulthood: The Winding Road from the Late Teens through the Twenties* (Oxford: Oxford University Press, 2004).

Rich Heffern's article "American Catholics: The 'Bookend' Generations," *National Catholic Reporter* (March 9, 2007), presents a very accessible analysis of generational differences and similarities among Catholics. Here he reviews and synopsizes research coordinated by sociologist William D'Antonio from 1987 to 2005 that studied pre– and post–Vatican II Catholic values and practices.

To view human sexuality from a feminist perspective, campus ministers would do well to consult Lisa Sowle Cahill's *Sex, Gender, and Christian Ethics* (Cambridge: Cambridge University Press, 1996).

Journalist Colleen Carroll, after interviewing young adults across the country, reports a turn toward traditional beliefs and morality in *The New Faithful: Why Young Adults Are Embracing Christian Orthodoxy* (Chicago: Loyola Press, 2002).

Donna Freitas takes a candid, in-depth look into the real lives of college students through their attitudes and experiences of sexuality and spirituality on secular and religious campuses in *Sex and the Soul: Juggling Sexuality, Spirituality, Romance, and Religion on America's College Campuses* (New York: Oxford University Press, 2008).

Sociologist Dean R. Hoge and colleagues explore beliefs, practices, and such attitudes as apathy among 848 individuals in *Young Adult Catholics: Religion in the Culture of Choice* (Notre Dame, IN: University of Notre Dame Press, 2001).

For a look at how a group of emerging adults in the new millennium search for spiritual meaning, read Christian Smith and Patricia Snell's *Souls in Transition: The Religious and Spiritual Lives of Emerging Adults* (Oxford: Oxford University Press, 2009).

To learn more about how Millennials (Generation Y-ers) are situated historically—as well as about their dominant attributes, values, and characteristics—read William Straus and Neil Howe's *Millennials Rising: The Next Great Generation* (London: Vintage Books, 2000).

An excellent executive summary of William Straus and Neil Howe's later book, *Millennials Go to College* (Washington, DC: American Association of Collegiate Registrars, 2003), can be found online at http://eubie.com/millennials.pdf. Prepared by Steve Eubanks of Azusa Pacific University, this four-page summary of the book captures the key attributes of the Generation Y-ers as these impact higher education in general.

CHAPTER THREE

ROLE OF THE CAMPUS MINISTER

HAVING LOOKED AT THE PROFILE of students on Catholic college campuses, we now turn our attention to the role of campus ministers in the twenty-first century. Because of the dramatic shift in the lived experience and faith perspective of young adults in the new millennium, campus ministers are now faced with the daunting challenge of adapting and adjusting their pastoral approaches to meet the signs of the times. Nearly forty-five years later, the words of the Second Vatican Council still ring true:

> The joys and the hopes, the griefs and the anxieties of the men and women of this age, especially those who are poor or in any way afflicted, these are the joys and hopes, the griefs and anxieties of the followers of Christ. Indeed, nothing genuinely human fails to raise an echo in their hearts.[1]

Hence, the change in roles for campus ministers implies a concomitant redefining of their identities as well as their practice of ministry in the twenty-first century to respond to the particular joys and hopes, griefs and anxieties of students on Catholic campuses. Let us now look at various aspects of campus ministry that reflect these changes in identity, theory, and approach.

Not uncommonly, campus ministers find themselves called upon to participate in crisis intervention in the student residence halls and other locations on campus. Frequently, sensitive incidents occur that reflect poor judgment on the part of students regarding the use of drugs or alcohol. Less often, students attempt or actually succeed in taking their own lives.[2] All of these situations (and others) necessitate involvement by campus ministers to intervene for the pastoral well-being of students, faculty, and staff. Although their role is not that of psychologists or social workers, campus ministers invest a great deal of time, often at ungodly hours, to console, accompany, and support those in crisis with pastoral care and prayer. This type of intervention entails many hours of stress-filled commitment to provide the special and appropriate kind of pastoral presence demanded of sensitive situations.

Due to their commitment to be present to those who are experiencing crises at Catholic colleges, campus ministers need to have a plan in place to address these urgent pastoral and spiritual needs. Certainly a team approach is most indicated, one in which ministers take turns to be on call to respond quickly and compassionately to these critical situations. In addition, professional training in grief counseling could prove quite beneficial for each member of the team. Finally, campus ministry can enhance its own effectiveness by coordinating with other campus agencies and departments, such as residence life and student affairs, as well as the campus counseling center, to develop a strategic plan for individual and community crisis intervention. Recognizing their own gifts and limitations, campus ministers can and should play a vital role in reaching out to students, faculty, and staff in times of grief, emergency, and disaster.

Another pastoral service that campus ministers typically provide is spiritual direction or spiritual guidance. To successfully perform this service, campus ministers should ideally have formal training and experience in individual spiritual direction practices, as well as in guiding groups of students and other adults in retreats and prayer services or liturgies. Many excellent centers around the United States offer yearly summer institutes for this purpose.[3] Other campus ministers may choose to specialize in this area during their graduate theological studies programs, which often require in-service training and mentoring in providing spiritual direction and giving retreats. Regardless of the program one might choose, additional training is needed in this area if campus ministers are to assist today's college students in making those challenging connections between faith and practice that are evidently lacking in the current generations of young adults.

Another aspect of the campus minister's role in the service of college students on Catholic campuses is pastoral counseling. Not to be confused with psychotherapy or psychological counseling, pastoral counseling is a form of confidential, individual guidance in regard to the everyday moral and spiritual life of a college student. Traditionally this has been looked upon as the role of the priest who gives "fatherly" spiritual advice to those who seek his good counsel. However, in the twenty-first century, this role is most often shared among women and men who form part of the campus ministry team; in addition, this role now takes on a number of new dimensions. Typical themes that surface in pastoral counseling are vocational discernment, relationship issues, sexual-orientation issues, family and roommate problems, as well as personal decision making and grieving. Sometimes a pastoral counseling session is a one-time event or opportunity to reach out to the college students. Other times, it could entail ongoing appointments as requested by the student or recommended by the campus minister.

Of course, special care needs to be taken to identify issues and concerns that are beyond the scope of pastoral counseling. In such instances, campus ministers would do well to have at their disposal the names and contact information of suitable psychologists and social workers who can more appropriately deal with problems beyond their own expertise as pastoral counselors. In any event, pastoral counseling should never presume to treat or diagnose the psychological or emotional problems of a college student.[4] In short, pastoral counseling is a form of spiritual conversation in which the young adult can voice some of his or her concerns and issues in a safe, personal environment, without the possible stigma that can be attributed to seeking out some form of therapy. Additional training for pastoral counseling can be sought through clinical pastoral education (CPE) programs or formal graduate courses at schools or departments of theology around the country.[5]

As suggested earlier in this chapter, many offices of campus ministry choose to take a team approach that allows them to tap into the various strengths, talents, and special training of the different women and men who serve as campus ministers. One clear benefit of such an approach is that no single campus minister has to bear the burden of being an expert in all areas of ministry. In fact, many teams prefer that each campus minister have a unique specialty such as marriage preparation, liturgical ministry, spiritual direction, or sacramental ministry as part of his or her formal educational or experiential background.

In addition to professional campus ministry staff, student volunteers assist in the various activities that this ministry entails. It is important to distinguish between those who have received professional training and formal education as campus ministers and those who have not, such as the student volunteers. Some aspects to consider when selecting student volunteers are their leadership ability, their interest in particular areas, such as social justice, liturgy, and music, and their special talents and gifts. In any case, student leaders need to be persons who are consistent and have a deep sense of commitment to campus ministry during their college years.

To achieve this level of student involvement in campus ministry, the professional team must develop, nurture, and mentor those students who have come forward to participate as leaders. One way to assist in this process is to have detailed job descriptions for student leaders so that expectations of their activities and commitment are made explicit. Another technique to foster their growth as leaders is to have them participate in monthly reflection sessions. Also, if these students are campus ministry interns, they should be paid hourly for the pastoral services they provide, as recognition of their dedication and commitment.

Since these student leaders are indeed the future leaders of the Church of tomorrow—especially in the areas of liturgy, social justice, faith formation, and interfaith issues—the professional campus ministers would be wise to invest a great deal of time and effort in training and mentoring them. Part of this training is ensuring that the student leaders can relate well to other people. One way to achieve this goal is to require that they participate in an overnight retreat prior to the beginning of classes to foster a spirit of prayer and collaboration in the formation of the team for the new academic year. Many Catholic colleges and universities have found that these student leaders are the ones who attract other students to attend the liturgies on Sunday evenings, as well as invite others to participate in various activities sponsored by campus ministry.

Returning our attention to the professional ministry staff, an essential consideration in developing a team is the recruitment, selection, and retention of highly qualified and gifted members. Some factors that staffs ought to take into account in this regard include their own staff needs and the possible necessity of conducting a nationwide or local search. Factors to look for in team members include an understanding of mission and identity or a willingness to grow in appreciation of it; and a comfortable fit with current staff; that is, the human dimension. Some duties or responsibilities that are most common among campus ministers at Catholic colleges and universities are pastoral counseling, grief counseling, spiritual guidance, retreat direction, liturgical ministry, sacramental ministry, and social-service project direction. It is recommended that teams take into account the particular skills that would complement those ministers already on staff. Although campus ministers are sometimes selected for their youthfulness and popular appeal, and other times for their experience and range of success, all applicants need formal training and certification[6] as campus ministry professionals. Another important aspect to include is a balance of gender, age, and ethnic diversity among team members to better serve the various needs of female and male students, as well as those from different cultural and religious backgrounds. As St. Paul emphasized, "There are different kinds of spiritual gifts but the same Spirit; there are different forms of service but the same Lord" (1 Cor 12:4–5).

Having a clear perspective of the context and mission of a particular college or university's campus ministry program is essential to the effective recruitment of new team members. One factor in this clarity of perspective is the size and environment of the Catholic institution. For example, some colleges or universities are in urban locations, while others are in suburban or small city environments. Still others have a student body that is composed of a majority of Catholics and other Christians; whereas some others are quite diverse in regard to religious and cultural pluralism. Even more uniquely, some Catholic institutions have either predominantly or exclusively one gender represented among those enrolled. Clearly, much care needs to be taken when recruiting campus ministers who will best fit the context and environment of each Catholic college or university, even while striving to provide a team that has a balance of representation of both men and women.

In addition to social and demographic considerations, when campus ministry staffs recruit new members for their teams, they need to keep in mind the charism of the religious order or diocese that founded the institution. Conversations with directors or vice presidents for mission and identity will assist the team in preparing their search. These discussions can yield interview questions that will help guide the recruiting process to take into account the particular spirituality or core religious values that are part of the mission of the college or university. Efforts to identify the kinds of perspectives and values a campus minister would have within this spiritual context will serve to clarify expectations on the part of both the campus ministry staff and the institution. Certainly, a solid theological grounding plus practical ministerial training should be part of the job description of a campus minister.

Of course, what is essential in campus ministers is a mature faith. This means a committed adult, whether priest, religious, or layperson, who lives out his or her adult spirituality authentically. Unfortunately, this has not always the case in the past, especially in the sixties and seventies, during and just after the Second Vatican Council. In addition, a campus minister needs to be a psychologically balanced individual (especially since he or she does spiritual direction and pastoral counseling). To that end, persons who are in training as campus ministers need professional education and pastoral experience. Holding a graduate degree such as an MDiv or MA in pastoral ministry is preferred. However, a person still working on such a degree could serve as an assistant campus minister, thereby allowing him or her to combine formal education with the requisite pastoral experience.

Other beneficial experiences or training might include service or work such as a Jesuit volunteer, youth minister, high school campus minister, or liturgy coordinator. Regardless of the type of pastoral experience they have had, candidates for campus ministry positions should have a real zeal or passion for what they are all about. It is also particularly helpful if college students are involved in the interview process when campus ministry hires a new team member to ensure that they relate to the contemporary scene. Since campus ministers need to be able to "connect" with the students and develop good personal relationships, care must be taken to verify that the candidates grasp twenty-first century college student reality, including knowledge of texting, tweeting, Facebook, and other technological media that are commonplace ways for young adults to communicate.[7] Recognizing the challenges of communicating in the postmodern age, Tim Muldoon succinctly elaborated that "we need to connect with other people around issues beyond everyday life."[8]

When searching for a director of campus ministry, interview teams should also insist on several years of prior experience in college-level campus ministry. Since we live in an outcome-assessment culture, the campus ministry team needs to have specific goals and ways of assessing them. Certainly, they should make sure that campus ministers are not stereotyped as merely "nice" people or always "yes" people.

It is essential for campus ministers to keep current in the latest trends in theology, spirituality, and religious education. Many opportunities for this are available to members of campus ministry teams.

Catholic Colleges in the 21st Century

Frequently, Catholic colleges and universities have extensive book and periodical selections for reading in their libraries, or even online. Some offer continuing education courses to employees through their theology and religious studies departments. Other campus ministry teams plan and organize their own staff development workshops and retreats, or tap into organizations such as the Catholic Campus Ministry Association (CCMA),[9] or their diocesan religious education conferences, for further professional development. Finally, since campus ministers provide spiritual guidance, they themselves need spiritual direction and personal retreats, and should attend workshops while on retreat, and so forth. The suggested readings at the end of each chapter will assist campus ministers with their ongoing professional development.

Depending upon the institution of higher education involved, campus ministry teams may require an MA for hall directors/ministers, and others a BA, looking for undergraduates with experience in campus ministry, and graduates with experience in parish, youth, and retreat ministries. In addition, the degree to which they can relate to a younger audience is essential to include along with academics: ultimately, the depth and quality of their experience is a significant factor.

Due to the economic downturn and the accompanying slowing of hiring in campus ministry, many teams currently have no formal training programs in place. Even so, campus ministry teams still have expectations of their colleagues in regard to training in Scripture, dogma, sacramental theology, pastoral counseling, spiritual/retreat direction, and youth ministry retreats; as well as credibility with faculty, parents, and the public at large, a grasp of academic experience, and his or her own life experience. Campus ministry budgets need to plan for salaries that appropriately compensate individuals for their expertise and training. In the past, many Catholic institutions of higher education were notoriously low in their salary levels. Much ongoing advancement work is needed to generate adequate internal and external funding if campus ministry offices are to recruit and retain quality people on their teams. Happily, many Catholic colleges and universities have already corrected historically inequitable salaries through such efforts.

Student leadership is an important element to consider in developing a link between campus ministry and student activities. In this regard, the importance of staff development and mentoring cannot be stressed enough. Key to this is identifying those talents needed to complement the team already in place. This requires having professionals on staff who have the appropriate academic credentials and who are men and women of deep personal faith. Training and forming future leaders is what campus ministry must do. We need to avoid developing a "cult mentality" among students involved in campus ministry. Students dealing with their peers are much more effective than professional staff in motivating and reaching college students. The ultimate aim is to provide guidance without being controlling.

Of course, when organizing and planning the scope of campus ministry, much depends on the size of the team. In any event, part of campus ministry's budget should provide for professional development: this entails attendance at workshops and conferences. For example, Dominican College in Florida provides an annual occasion for people in Catholic campus ministry to exchange ideas, to assess and compare programs, and to do some professional updating. Membership in appropriate campus ministry organizations needs to be encouraged. Areas that need to be covered and updated are gender balance, as well as experience in faith and justice issues. Campus ministers should be able to work with the local religious communities and diocesan clergy to invite them to participate in events and discussions. If possible, non-Catholics should be included on the team, and the team should brainstorm on how to reach out to non-Catholics on campus. An example of this is providing Bible study discussions, especially since the Scriptures do not belong solely to Protestants. Ideally, the campus ministry team should also build bridges with already-existing pastoral resources in the surrounding community and neighborhood.

RECOMMENDED READING

Drawing upon their experience in working with young adults in Chicago and directing young adult ministry there, John Cusick and Katherine Devries provide a good resource for program ideas in *The Basic Guide to Young Adult Ministry* (Maryknoll, NY: Orbis, 2001).

Margaret Farley, a renowned Roman Catholic feminist ethicist, presents a framework for sexual ethics based on justice in her book *Just Love: A Framework for Christian Sexual Ethics* (New York: Continuum, 2006).

Executive director of the Association of Catholic Colleges and Universities, Alice Gallin is the editor of a volume that collects twenty-five years of documents tracing the history of Catholic higher education in the United States since Vatican II: *American Catholic Higher Education: Essential Documents, 1967–1990* (Notre Dame: University of Notre Dame Press, 1993). This reference book is of particular interest for those investigating details of *Ex Corde Ecclesiae* and other developments that affect the Catholic identity of colleges and universities.

To more thoroughly study the historical developments and changes in campus ministry in the United States, read Michael Galligan-Stierle, ed., *The Gospel on Campus: A Handbook of Campus Ministry Programs and Resources*, 2nd ed. (Washington, DC: USCCB Publishing, 1996).

For a traditional Catholic commentary on human sexuality and sexual behavior among young adults, some may appreciate David Hajduk's perspective in *God's Plan for You: Life, Love, Marriage, and Sex (The Theology of the Body for Young People)* (Boston: Pauline Books & Media, 2006).

For a balanced, popular study of the cultural context of young adults and their faith, as well as insights into young adult ministry, read Michael Hayes's *Googling God: Landscape of People in Their 20s and 30s* (Mahwah, NJ: Paulist Press, 2007).

Campus ministers, and others involved in the distinctive nature of Catholic mission and identity, can find a wealth of information in Thomas C. Hunt, ed., *Handbook of Research on Catholic Higher Education* (Charlotte, NC: Information Age Publishing, 2003).

Viewing Catholic colleges and universities from the perspective of organizational culture, Melanie M. Morey and John J. Piderit, SJ, describe the present situation and offer concrete suggestions for enhancing Catholic identity, culture, and mission in *Catholic Higher Education: A Culture in Crisis* (New York: Oxford University Press, 2006).

For an overview of the historical, social, and theological development of campus ministry, see the National Catholic Conference of Bishops, *Empowered by the Spirit: Campus Ministry Faces the Future* (Washington, DC: National Catholic Conference of Bishops, 1985).

For a clear vision and plan of action for campus ministry across the country, read the United States Conference of Catholic Bishops, *Empowering Campus Ministry* (Washington, DC: USCCB Publishing, 2002), which builds upon their previous document *Empowered by the Spirit* (1985).

Drawing upon Pope John Paul II's theology of the body, Christopher West presents a clear and concise summary of Catholic teaching about sexuality and marriage in *The Good News about Sex and Marriage: Answers to Your Honest Questions about Catholic Teaching* (Ann Arbor, MI: Servant Publications, 2004).

CHAPTER FOUR

ACADEMIC LIFE AND CAMPUS MINISTRY

IN APRIL 2010, FATHER ADOLFO NICOLÁS, the superior general of the Society of Jesus, addressed more than two hundred presidents of Jesuit universities and colleges from around the world. In his address to the delegates, Father Nicolás commented on the world scene as he perceived it, especially as it impacts higher education. His audience consisted of representatives from the largest Catholic university "system" on this planet. His remarks are worth quoting somewhat at length since they focus on both the theoretical and the practical.

Father Nicolás stated:

> Our globalized world has seen the spread of two rival "ism's": on the one hand, a dominant "world culture" is marked by an aggressive secularism that claims that faith has nothing to say to the world and its great problems (and which often claims that religion, in fact, is one of the world's great problems); on the other hand, the resurgence of various fundamentalisms, often fearful or angry reactions to postmodern world culture, which escape complexity by taking refuge in a certain "faith" divorced from or unregulated by human reason. And, as Pope Benedict points out, both "secularism and fundamentalism exclude the possibility of fruitful dialogue and effective cooperation between reason and religious faith."[1]

Given that situation, Nicolás pointed out that research should be "aimed at making a difference in people's lives, rather than simply a recondite conversation among members of a closed elite group."[2]

What results should be expected from a Catholic education? Father Nicolás said:

> Whether our students are being transformed—this also has to be evaluated. How do they perform later?...Do they collaborate when some of the issues in which we are involved bring conflict with the government, when this might bring some weakening in the profits they make in the companies?[3]

Both Pope Benedict XVI and Father Nicolás address a situation that is not isolated to Jesuit institutions. With what concrete actions do institutions of higher education address the needs of the changing global situation? What are some recent precedents for a more collaborative approach between the intellectual and the practical? In a sense, academic life and campus ministry are but two sides of the same coin. They complement rather than oppose each other.

Although an institution of higher education operates as a whole, nevertheless, each of its various employees has a different job description. For instance, teachers have contracts that spell out responsibilities. Faculty members are held accountable for meeting students and covering material of a certain, definable area. They do this by teaching the students formally for a certain number of times during the semester or quarter in a classroom setting, holding office hours, and periodically attending staff meetings at which they discuss issues such as curriculum, ways to make the department run more smoothly, and so on. Usually at the end of the course, the institution asks the students to evaluate the performance of their teachers. These evaluations often count much toward a teacher's promotion, salary, and tenure. In a similar manner, evaluations are essential to those who are part of the campus ministry team.

Campus ministry provides the practical applications of what is learned formally in the classroom. Thus, a campus ministry team needs to adapt itself to the academic structure. In practical terms, this arrangement means that scheduling events can be difficult because many people have so many diverse commitments. Students' and professors' schedules always have priority. On a positive note, however, campus ministry programs can be geared to giving more attention to individuals and small groups.

Relationships between faculty members and campus ministry teams have not always been smooth. When we look at campus ministry from a historical perspective, we have frequently seen poorly funded offices, personnel who have little appreciation for college academic life, almost no job descriptions, and positions whose very purpose of existence is undefined. In fact, when campus ministry first began, faculty and administrators frequently tolerated rather than promoted it. Some of these elements are still found today. Additionally, certain prejudices have existed on the part of faculty members who had little use for any office that was not strictly academic. They viewed activities sponsored by campus ministry as just more instances of institutions providing unneeded distractions for students.

Since Vatican II, however, some natural changes have evolved. Faculty members and members of campus ministry teams have both realized that hands-on experiences enhance education. Catholic educators frequently state that they want to educate "the whole person," something to which Father Nicolás speaks.

As mentioned in chapter 1, the Catholic educators who met in 1967 at Land O' Lakes advocated that colleges and universities encourage programs where students can

> experiment further in Christian service by undertaking activities embodying the Christian interest in all human

problems—inner-city social action, personal aid to the educationally disadvantaged, and so forth.

Thus will arise within the Catholic university a self-developing and self-deepening society of students and faculty in which the consequences of Christian truth are taken seriously in person-to-person relationships, where the importance of religious commitment is accepted and constantly witnessed to, and where the students can learn by personal experience to consecrate their talent and learning to worthy social purposes.

All of this will display itself on the Catholic campus as a distinctive style of living, a perceptible quality in the university's life.[4]

Almost a quarter century later, Pope John Paul II spelled out more fully the same necessity of such a mutual interchange between theory and practice when he said:

Pastoral ministry is that activity of the University which offers the members of the university community an opportunity to integrate religious and moral principles with their academic study and non-academic activities, *thus integrating faith with life.* . . .

Those involved in pastoral ministry will encourage teachers and students to become more aware of their responsibility toward those who are suffering physically or spiritually. Following the example of Christ, they will be particularly attentive to the poorest and to those who suffer economic, social, cultural or religious injustice. This responsibility begins within the academic community, but it also finds application beyond it. (*Ex Corde Ecclesiae*, nos. 38 and 40; emphasis in the original)

Catholic Colleges in the 21st Century

Although carrying out such holistic experiences sometimes involves different interpretations of the institution's mission statement, nevertheless, agreements usually outweigh the differences and disagreements. Let us consider three areas:

Catholic colleges and universities are interested in critical reflection. This wide category looks at specific disciplines, as well as examines the sociopolitical atmospheres in which people act and live. Critical reflection challenges people to ask themselves: "Where do I stand on various issues? Emotionally? Intellectually?" Such questions imply that people know the presuppositions of issues (for example, what do people assume when they hear someone say that laziness is the cause of disparity in the distribution of wealth?) and that they then reflect on the various factors involved before they draw their conclusions. We do not really fully educate people if they simply memorize material, but cannot contextualize it (or even internalize it). Campus ministry helps students do this by providing the forum and the accompanying experiences that can facilitate students, faculty, and others to examine critically such questions from a religious perspective. Campus ministry also gives people additional data they can use in making important and fully informed decisions.

Since we do not think or act in a vacuum, the second area in which campus ministry implements a Catholic institution's vision is to highlight the role of our relationships to others. Catholics take seriously Jesus' injunction, "Love your neighbor as yourself" (Matt 19:19). Jesus gave a good example of how this could be done in the first century when he was asked: "Who is my neighbor?" He replied by telling the story of the Good Samaritan (Luke 10:30–37). In that example, a member of a minority class took care of a stranger who had been robbed and beaten while traveling. The Samaritan used some of his own funds to help the victim, while others from the religious establishment passed by without providing any aid. Today, in the era of globalization, we realize that we are linked to our neighbors just as the Samaritan was to the stranger he happened upon. We too can pass by our neighbor or we can help in diverse ways. Catholic institutions of higher education stress that people's talents are not just for their own self-enrichment, but they are to be used for the good of others. How are we Good Samaritans in practice?

Certainly this role is something that faculty and staff can discuss at an academic level, but campus ministry has a unique opportunity to facilitate helping one's neighbor experientially in situations where people realize their responsibilities to others, as well as their obligation to take care of God's creation for present and future generations. Examples include not only sponsoring CYO Search Retreats, but also organizing opportunities for doing volunteer work. A project such as serving in a soup kitchen should cause people in the college community to question the root of such economic disparity and, following the example of the Good Samaritan, motivate them to work to remove the root cause of the problem, in addition to consider how to set up different, more just structures for the future.

A third and obvious area where campus ministry plays a vital role in a college environment is that of deepening people's faith. On campuses, especially those that are pluralistic and diverse, this means making a special effort to reach out to those who are not Catholics. Often enough this also entails explaining to Catholics the basics of their faith. All people seek answers to questions such as these: Who are we? What is the meaning of life? What is moral good (and moral evil)? Why does suffering exist? What is true happiness? Is there life after death? From the time when the first human being made an appearance on this planet until now, people have taken various approaches to answer these questions. Their responses have been conditioned over the centuries by the cultures in which they live, by historical events, and by some types of value systems. These issues arise on the college campus both in courses and in less formal encounters. No simple answers exist: a certain ambiguity surrounds all of us. Campus ministry can be of assistance to people who are living with this ambiguity by helping them to understand their religious beliefs better, as well as ways of acting according to those beliefs. The challenge to campus ministry is how to do this in a meaningful way. The campus ministry team must ask itself: What programs best help us examine our faith commitment and then deepen it?

Campus ministry is successful when it has helped people (1) approach life with a critical mind, (2) realize that life is not lived in a vacuum, (3) actively show concern for others, and (4) deepen their faith.

A college or university's mission and vision is carried out through the school's core curriculum. The core curriculum specifies basic skills and outcomes that the institution wants the students to have at the end of an undergraduate program of studies. A glance at the institution's core curriculum is usually enough to see what degree of religious literacy the graduate is expected to have at the undergraduate level. How many courses are required? Can a graduating senior articulate how the courses relate to the world and individuals? Is the graduate acquainted with ethics and able to apply it to daily life?

When members of the campus ministry team look at the number of required courses in a given institution, they have a basic profile of the students' current preparation. If there are few theology or religious studies courses, then the campus ministry team will need to deal with that limitation. An added issue is that students often postpone enrolling in required courses until their junior or senior years. Thus, they often have had very few encounters in the classroom with theology and religious studies courses until they are close to graduation. A religious common ground during the undergraduate years frequently does not exist. Those who are hiring the staff of campus ministry will need to select people who can provide the basics to those students who have not fulfilled any "prerequisites." The diversity of students' backgrounds underscores the need for the campus ministry team to reflect this same diversity if it is to be effective.

One religious phenomenon in the contemporary U.S. culture continues to be the emphasis on an individual's relationship to God. That approach coincides with the "rugged individualism" that has been one of the country's key ideas over the last two centuries. People boast that they can get ahead in life by their own brains, hard work, and ingenuity. This has sometimes happened at the expense of their neighbors and the common good. Such an attitude is frequently observed when people declare they are spiritual yet do not formally belong to any organized religion. Even though many of them have been baptized into a certain faith community, often they are part of that community only in name, not in practice. Yet since Vatican II and the advent of globalization, organized religion is changing. Among students today, no matter what their religion, most of them see the necessity of a personal commitment to the betterment of their neighbor if the world itself is to survive.

Historically, most colleges and universities have encouraged students to use their intellectual talents for the benefit of others. Law students can help those with immigration problems; business majors can advise minority firms; nursing, medical, and dental students can do much pro bono work; and those who major in liberal arts can tutor those in need of individual instruction. Campus ministry can provide the context for reflection for all this: our lives are lived in relationships. We need to realize both emotionally and physically that we do not live in a vacuum, but then we must put our realizations into action. Campus ministry can not only build on programs that already exist, but also lead people to examine how these programs address issues that are based in a larger context. No one can deny that in today's international political world, religion plays a big role. Campus ministry can provide cross-disciplinary reflection by cooperating with already-existing courses and programs.

Today's students frequently do not want to be in an atmosphere that is "too churchy." They have sometimes seen blindness in those in charge of various faith communities who theoretically have a "higher" viewpoint, but which sometimes turns out to be very narrow. Today's students do not want to be totally identified with attending services on a regular basis or to appear to be too pious. A middle path exists, however. By its very name, campus ministry looks to the development of the whole person. That includes both the intellectual and the spiritual. If a college or university wants students, faculty, and staff to see their relationship to others, part of that relationship necessarily involves the worship community. Formal religious practice can be made attractive if the campus ministry team invests time in its preparation. Not every community worships the same way, but a college or university usually has many factors that help enhance and provide a successful worship atmosphere. Some of these features are common age groups, common interests, common classes and experiences, and a common geography (working or living on campus or within an easy commute). Similar elements have made the parish system so successful among Catholics (which often has the added advantage of common socioeconomic class and even ethnicity). Formal worship on college campuses can and should be focused on the immediate participants. That means that campus ministry needs to provide worship opportunities that are geared to students, faculty, and staff.

Since members of the campus ministry team are educators in a special way, they can use liturgies to provide both devotional and educational opportunities. Let us take the Mass as an example. Some of the elements involved are the readings from Scripture, the homily, and the music. Toward the end of the Mass, people are invited to break bread together and drink from the same cup. They proclaim their common humanity and faith, and their bonds with each other. The Scripture passages read earlier in the Mass provide connections to the past. We cannot control what happened centuries ago, but we do need to know how our Judeo-Christian heritage was formed. How are we living in continuity with our common past? How has the Bible influenced the arts, legal systems, human rights, and so on, of Western civilization? Some knowledge of the Bible is necessary for anyone to have had a liberal education, since it cuts across ages and cultures. The one who gives the homily has a wonderful opportunity to apply some of the biblical lessons and experiences to current circumstances. This is an excellent chance to educate and motivate those in attendance. Over the course of a semester, the topics can be as diverse as questions of justice, relationships, value systems, and moral codes. Hence, the Mass provides a chance for people to learn as well as to show their devotion. Good music, Martin Luther once said, enhances the words. (Of course, bad music can do the opposite.) Thus, the music at Mass can be an added aid. At Mass, Catholics meditate on the meaning of Jesus' death and resurrection, and the impact it has had, is having, and will have in the future. The world is different because of Christianity. That different world includes the role of colleges and universities.

Along with the Mass, there are other worshiping and learning opportunities. The Rite of Christian Initiation of Adults (RCIA) is a process that takes place over several months. This particular program is easily adapted to local contexts. Its purpose is to prepare people to be received into the Catholic Church. Also invited to participate in the program are those Catholics who have been baptized but have never practiced or been brought up in the faith. Practicing Catholics sometimes join the program just to learn more about their faith. The RCIA introduces people as a group to Catholic theology and Church practices, especially as they relate to the various ceremonies and sacraments. For instance, the group might attend the first part of a Mass and then break for a discussion on the Scripture readings. Over a period of months, various professors from theology and religious studies departments might spend an evening with the group and talk on their expertise. This holistic approach takes in experiences, formal presentations, and discussion. Campus ministry is uniquely situated to provide this program. The beauty of this is that it simultaneously involves a cross-section of people in the college (faculty, staff, and students). These groups all share in a common experience that is both intellectual and religious.

Retreats offer another opportunity for campus ministry to be effective. Retreats usually involve several people who leave the physical environment of the campus as a group to spend time in prayer and reflection. Those in charge of the retreat provide direction and goals.

The focus is to find God in one's personal life (which involves living in a community). This means setting aside time for personal prayer and having a chance to be away from telephones, computers, and outside cares and distractions. Retreats go by different names, depending on their emphasis. Each has a different format but ultimately the purpose is to bring people closer to God in the context in which they live and work. In sponsoring retreat programs, campus ministry helps people to integrate their daily lives with their religious beliefs.

Sometimes campus ministry can't plan ahead for all the opportunities for involvement. For instance, an unplanned discussion group can complement class discussions. Obviously topics in morality and ethics are issues in which people have much interest. For example, people wonder why they shouldn't download music from the Internet without paying. On the other hand, planned discussion groups are also effective. Surprisingly, reading the Bible is a practice that enjoys much popularity. People usually haven't read the Bible, or if they have, they have done so from a fundamentalist rather than critical viewpoint. Sometimes they discover that a whole new world exists.

Up to this point, we have mentioned areas in which a campus ministry team deals with groups of people. Not everything, however, can and should be handled with a whole group present. What about an individual who wants some privacy? Sincere people want to integrate their relationships to each other and to God. Thus, campus ministry needs to provide individual spiritual direction to students, staff, and faculty. These latter two groups are more likely to seek personal spiritual direction on a continuing basis than are students. Still, most people prefer to bounce ideas off someone else and get another viewpoint on where they are spiritually. Spiritual direction and pastoral counseling are areas where campus ministry can make substantial contributions.

The whole ambience of a college is educational. Much of it is done in a formal way through classroom instruction; sometimes, however, people learn as much or more in informal meetings, conversations, and groups than in the actual classroom. Since campus ministry must work with class schedules in mind, members of the team must be available at odd hours. Having a cup of coffee between classes with one or more students can sometimes turn into a real learning experience for all the parties involved. People are in a place where they can freely express their feelings. If people differ from each other in ethnicity or religion, the conversation can become very enlightening on almost any subject. With campus ministry's presence, people's concerns will undoubtedly touch on religion in some form or another. Likewise, if one or more members of the campus ministry team live in the residence halls, they will have an influence on those with whom they come into contact. Some schools have "living/learning" communities so that there is continuity between the classroom and where one lives. Learning does not stop when one leaves the classroom.

If campus ministry is the main vehicle that a college or university uses to provide a Catholic presence in the institution, then those working for campus ministry do not have a nine-to-five job. It could be better described as one that observes a 24/7 schedule. Members of the team do not always have the luxury of leaving the campus and not returning until the next day. For instance, a team member who has organized an evening discussion group becomes sick and needs a substitute; a student is arrested and wants help; a group from outside the campus is on the property passing out literature that attacks the college and the Church. Events like these happen at every institution and demand an immediate response. These are also times when campus ministry needs to show a presence. Showing care and concern for others is what Catholic institutions should be all about, and can be demonstrated concretely in such situations by campus ministry.

Many schools were founded by members of religious orders and congregations. Frequently enough, that initial charism is still found among the institutions today even though the number of religious men and women is minimal. For example, the twenty-eight Jesuit colleges and universities in the United States follow the 450-year-old inspiration of St. Ignatius Loyola that we should aim to find God in all things, and that we should educate the whole person—spiritually, intellectually, and morally. In Jesuit schools, this is most often reflected in the curriculum, which usually includes mandatory courses in ethics and theology. Campus ministry can translate similar charisms into everyday life.

Today, colleges frequently orient students to the world rather than focus them on just their own academic disciplines. Schools promote slogans like "Make the difference," "Be the change," and so on. This does not diminish the importance of the work that people are doing in fields like engineering and physics, to give just two examples. At first glance, these fields seem like unlikely areas for people to effect directly some type of social change in the world. But then we realize how engineering has shaped the world with the construction of homes, dams, and highways. Physics has dominated the nuclear age and the whole space industry. When we look at these areas, we realize that concomitant moral and ethical issues arise especially in an era of globalization. These issues need to be pondered and discussed while students are in their college years. They need to discover—now—the side effects of how "for-profits" or "enlightened self-interest" influence the way people's expertise is used. What effect does this have on other people and generations to come? Areas such as media studies have great potential to influence large groups with attitudes of selfishness or generosity.

In all these examples, we see the importance of looking at Jesus' response to the person who asked him: "Who is my neighbor?" Campus ministry has the unique opportunity to apply to a college environment Jesus' response in the parable of the Good Samaritan. This response has not only an academic context but usually a living situation. As a result of the role that campus ministry plays in the formation of students, staff, and faculty, it is hoped that most will move to the next level of engagement that complements the theory learned in the classroom.

RECOMMENDED READING

Although "Empowered by the Spirit: Campus Ministry Faces the Future" is somewhat dated (the document was issued by the United States Conference of Catholics Bishops in 1985), it shows some of the earlier hopes and evaluations of campus ministry. It can be viewed at http://www.nccbuscc.org/education/highered/empowered.shtml.

Jessica Schubmehl, Stephen Cubbellotti, and William Van Ornum present a short but interesting discussion on "The Effect of Spirituality and Campus Ministry on Academic Accomplishment in College Students" at http://www.thefreelibrary.com/The+effect+of+spirituality+and+campus+ministry+on+academic...-a0207643304. This article is very limited in scope but does provide material for further consideration.

Thomas Morris gives a good overview of the RCIA program in *The RCIA: Transforming the Church* (Mahwah, NJ: Paulist Press, 1997).

For those interested in leading discussions on the Bible, Raymond Brown gives a good overview in his book *The Critical Meaning of the Bible* (Mahwah, NJ: Paulist Press, 1981).

Richard Gula situates the role of religious faith in making decisions in *Reason Informed by Faith: Foundations of Catholic Morality* (Mahwah, NJ: Paulist Press, 1989).

CHAPTER FIVE

STUDENT ACTIVITIES AND CAMPUS MINISTRY

IN THE PREVIOUS CHAPTER WE discussed the impact that campus ministry has on the academic life of students and faculty. Now we turn our attention to other activities, both cocurricular and extracurricular, that have a relationship with campus ministry. To begin with, one might wonder just how service-learning and volunteerism relate to campus ministry. To answer this query, we need to grasp the nature of these two types of cocurricular activities; namely, their particular characteristics and purposes.

A great deal of groundwork in this area has been done by Janet Eyler and Dwight E. Giles in their 1999 study entitled *Where's the Learning in Service-Learning?* They indicate that, although true service-learning experiences are extremely diverse, we can sense some common elements that run through all such experiences. Most service-learning experiences are "positive, meaningful and real to the participants...involve cooperative rather than competitive experiences...[and] address complex problems in complex settings rather than simplified problems in isolation." In addition, Eyler and Giles refer to the opportunities that service-learning experiences offer participants by engaging them in problem-solving activities in order to encourage them "to gain knowledge of the specific context of their service-learning activity and community challenges, rather than only to draw upon generalized or abstract knowledge such as might come from a textbook." All of this results in fostering the acquisition of critical thinking skills about real-life situations. In addition, service-learning motivates students because it engages them in a personal, meaningful, and emotional way "to challenge values as well as ideas, and hence to support social, emotional and cognitive learning and development."[1]

What is unique about service-learning is the way in which it enhances the community through the services rendered, even while it supports powerful learning outcomes for the participants. In the foreword to Eyler and Giles's book, Alexander Astin stated that "cognitive learning and affective service can be closely connected and thereby mutually reinforcing and that an affective outcome like commitment to service also has important cognitive components."[2] One of the reasons that service-learning has grown so quickly is the dynamic impact it has had on young people in regard to their emotional and cognitive development. As Eyler and Giles stress: "Experience enhances understanding; understanding leads to more effective action....Service-learning is a teaching and learning strategy that integrates meaningful community service with instruction and reflection to enrich the learning experience, teach civic responsibility, and strengthen communities."[3] Andrew Furco adds that it is equally important to point out that "service-learning programs are distinguished from other approaches to experiential education by their intention to equally benefit the provider and the recipient of the service, as well as to ensure equal focus on both the service being provided and the learning that is occurring."[4]

What role, then, does service-learning play in the curriculum at Catholic colleges and universities across the country? To get a sense of this, we can look at a sampling of general education program administrators who participated in a survey conducted by the Association of American Colleges and Universities (AAC&U) in late 2008 and early 2009. According to the results of their study, "when [college administrators were] asked about trends in the curricular practices at their institutions over the past five years...service learning in courses (68%) and internships (62%)...are high on the list."[5] Of course, this sample includes not only Catholic institutions of higher education, but other private and public ones as well.

Historically, campus ministry teams initiated volunteer or service activities and projects. In general, as these types of activities developed and became more popular, they were brought under the direction of student development offices or volunteer centers. Some campus ministry teams still maintain guidance over a few key volunteer experiences, such as School of the Americas trips or March for Life rallies. However, most others have been assumed under the supervision of other college or university offices. This change is due in part to administrative load and time constraints, as well as to the nature and scope of activities that best lend themselves to faith and justice experiences.

An important distinction should be made here between faith-based service experiences and community-outreach experiences. Although both have the common goal of improving conditions for the sake of social justice, community service or outreach lacks the faith-reflection dimension that is integral to any service-learning and immersion opportunities sponsored or cosponsored by campus ministry offices. Today's emerging adults are highly motivated toward service in the community, but all too frequently lack the tools necessary to integrate these experiences into their faith life as well as into their spirituality. "Emerging adults seek an educational experience that supports their exploration for meaning and purpose in vocation, personal relationships and civic responsibilities."[6]

Through the efforts of campus ministry professionals, students on Catholic college campuses have access to the guidance and encouragement they need to reflect upon their service experiences from a faith perspective. Campus ministers need to work in collaboration with student affairs professionals at Catholic colleges and universities, because good practice for student affairs not only "enriches student integration of faith and reason through the provision of co-curricular learning opportunities," but also "creates opportunities for students to experience, reflect upon, and act from a commitment to justice, mercy, and compassion, and in light of Catholic social teaching to develop respect and responsibility for all, especially those most in need."[7]

As we have seen in the current popularity of service-learning, the early part of the twenty-first century has also witnessed an increase in college students volunteering their time for service work. In fact, according to *College Students Helping America,* a report published by the Corporation for National and Community Service, college student volunteering increased by 20 percent between 2002 and 2005, more than doubling the growth in the adult volunteering rate. It found that 3.3 million college students volunteered in 2005—nearly 600,000 more students than three years ago—building strong momentum toward a national goal of five million college student volunteers by 2010.[8] Analysts have attributed this dramatic rise in civic engagement in part to the 9/11 attacks. Drawing conclusions based upon figures from the U.S. Census Bureau and the Bureau of Labor Statistics, the report includes a state-by-state ranking of college student volunteering. In particular, the study points to some key findings of interest to our discussion of student activities and campus ministry:

> Tutoring and mentoring are the most popular volunteer activities among college students. Among college student volunteers, tutoring (26.6%) and mentoring (23.8%) are the most popular volunteer activities. [It was also found that] 39.2 percent of black college student volunteers engage in mentoring activities, compared to 22.3 percent of white college student volunteers.[9]

One essential consideration in all of these efforts at working for social justice is how to ensure that experiences of service-learning, volunteer projects, and immersion opportunities are integrated with a faith-reflection component that, in turn, relates to Catholic social teaching. Another important factor to consider is the way in which the experiences can be imbued with the particular charism of the sponsoring religious congregation or diocese. Service for service's sake can no longer be the preferred approach of Catholic colleges and universities; rather, campus ministry must insist on the service of faith and the promotion of justice. Indeed, many of the Catholic institutions of higher education seek not only to learn from the poor and marginalized, but also to learn together with them. Ultimately, campus ministry teams should be the vanguard of such efforts.

Placing service-learning, volunteer programs, and immersion experiences under the direction of offices of student affairs could run the risk of secularizing these opportunities or denuding them of the faith-reflection dimension. In extreme cases, such programs begrudgingly accept the Catholic values espoused by the institution so as to justify them in the eyes of the vice president or director of mission and identity. This might even result in an additional disjointing between the mission and vision of the Catholic institution of higher education on the one hand and the lived experience of the students on the other. To remedy this potential downfall, campus ministry should play a key role in fostering the faith-reflection dimension of these efforts as a way of assisting students to integrate Catholic core values into their curricular and cocurricular experiences.

On another note, some leaders who oversee immersion experiences do not have the training or background experience necessary to guide college students in making the connections between their lived experiences and their faith. One potential role for campus ministry teams would be to offer training and professional-development workshops to help these leaders cultivate talents and abilities to direct faith-based reflection among students immersed in another context.

Immersion experiences are popular service opportunities among many college students, such as the program run by "Engineering beyond Borders," as well as others sponsored by Catholic colleges and universities, as we mentioned in chapter 1. These types of experiences frequently are seen as a way to challenge students to confront the realities of the world as well as reflect on their personal values. In particular, college students are confronted with the issues of poverty and injustice by being immersed into a cultural context different from their own. Such experiences often lead individuals to a deeper integration of their own faith and sense of personal vocation through critical reflection sessions before, during, and after the immersions.

These extracurricular events are college-sponsored trips for groups of students to locations within and outside the United States. Most of these excursions are of short duration ranging from one week to one month and might even entail some kind of service-learning. Frequently these experiences involve immersion not only in a unique cultural milieu but also in a foreign language context. Hence, some participants have the goal of practicing a second or third language as well as being exposed to a culture different from their own. In short, an immersion experience obligates the college student to step outside of his or her comfort zone to interface with the nitty-gritty world beyond the confines of their campus lifestyle enclave.[10]

One might well ask, just what is the relationship between campus ministry and these immersion programs? Certainly, by their very nature, these experiences involve college students who are highly motivated by certain altruistic, if not religious, values. Although the primary purpose of such an experience may be their own learning, college students most often intend to provide service or help to people in an area of particular need in their own country or in another. Immersion experiences have placed college students in Appalachia, New Orleans, Belize, Cuba, Mexico, El Salvador, South Africa, and other sites. Due to both the contexts of these immersions and the motivations of the college students, these programs and experiences provide an excellent opportunity for campus ministers to get involved, especially in designing and conducting the faith reflection components that are typically built into the programming of these events. By extension, these immersion experiences can be grounded in a critical pedagogy, which Ira Shor described as

> habits of thought, reading, writing, and speaking which go beneath the surface meaning, first impressions, dominant myths, official pronouncements, traditional clichés, received wisdom, and mere opinions, to understand the deep meaning, root causes, social context, ideology, and personal con-

sequences of any action, event, object, process, organization, experience, text, subject matter, policy, mass media, or discourse.[11]

In part, that is why faculty members and advisors across the country encourage their college students to participate in immersion programs, which are often described as life-altering experiences. Key to sorting out such experiences are the faith- and critical-reflection components. Campus ministry teams need to play a role in developing techniques and training to equip faculty and advisors to help students sort out these rich experiences from a faith perspective. To accomplish this, campus ministry teams would do well to educate themselves about the range of immersion opportunities available through their Catholic college or university. Furthermore, campus ministers could benefit from playing a role as advisors to these programs by serving on committees to oversee and evaluate the programs. Becoming more conscious of the various aspects of immersion placements, and even joining in these trips, campus ministers can more readily devise and develop curricular and cocurricular events to assist in the faith reflection component so necessary to them. Clearly, campus ministers need to participate in their own continuing education and workshops in order to keep up with current trends.

Most of these types of immersion programs began in the 1970s as a result of efforts to link social concern and consciousness with actual experiences in the contexts under study. Initially, offices of campus ministry promoted these efforts, only to later defer the oversight of them to student affairs or the offices of academic deans. This has resulted in a weakening of the faith-reflection components of these programs at some Catholic campuses. Campus ministry teams can and should take a more active role in promoting the integration of their core values and faith perspectives into these experiences.

One example of how campus ministers can work together with these immersion programs can be found at Santa Clara University, where such activities are housed under the Ignatian Center, whose purpose is to promote the Jesuit/Catholic mission. The campus ministry staff supports the Ignatian Center by providing students with reflection opportunities before, during, and after the immersions. Frequently someone from campus ministry accompanies the students on these experiences. Although social justice is already a predominant feature in many of the organizations and clubs at SCU, campus ministry offers to take the lead in guiding the reflections at their meetings.

Other settings that lend themselves to participation by campus ministry are intentional living communities or residence living communities, which are organized around common academic, cultural, and social interests. They consist of a group of students who choose to live together for a particular purpose, to share common goals, to commit to working together toward these goals, and to abide by the standards set forth and approved by residence life offices. Here the real challenge to campus ministry is to identify how the team might participate in the activities of these intentional living communities. In addition, taking into account the core values of their particular college or university, campus ministers will need to clarify the type of relationships they can develop with student or residence life personnel. Clarifying these relationships will help determine the extent and nature of campus ministry's participation in intentional living communities.

One potentially beneficial way for campus ministry to have a role in the tenor of living communities is to participate in the selection and/or training of hall ministers. This would first require conversations with residence life and student affairs personnel to determine how such a role might develop. Certainly the campus ministers who participate in the selection of hall ministers can lend their expertise in looking for the types of values and gifts necessary in such residence hall ministers who can assist college students in making connections between their faith and their living experiences. This role would serve to underscore the importance of a clearly articulated mission-and-vision statement that promotes the core values of the Catholic institution. Such a collaborative engagement by campus ministers could foster a spirit of camaraderie and a more holistic perspective on how to care for the emerging adults who live on campus or nearby.

Even though a residence hall may not be an intentional living community as such, it still would benefit from the involvement of campus ministry professionals. The influence that campus ministers have can be direct or indirect; they can actually live among the student residence halls as members of the campus ministry team or help train and select the hall ministers who live there. In either event, campus ministry's presence in this arena of the college students' experience is essential if teams are to approach their service in a holistic fashion; that is, to envision campus ministry as not just liturgical and sacramental service, but also service of the faith in all contexts of campus life.

Regardless of the various types of immersion experiences and intentional living communities, campus ministers often surface the issue of how to integrate faith reflection into these experiences. Furthermore, many ministers question how well these programs integrate the core values of the Catholic college or university into their content and planning. Clearly, dialogue about ways of integrating core values is essential in order to disambiguate campus ministry's role in the Catholic mission of the college or university. In addition, consideration needs to be made of the students' adult developmental needs with special regard to diversity of cultural and religious backgrounds. Of course, all of these values are dependent upon the student context and campus culture that vary from institution to institution.

Finally, campus ministry teams should review and evaluate their engagement with student life on a periodic basis. This could take the form of an annual program assessment much as those conducted by many academic units or departments. Feedback on service and immersion experiences by means of surveys of students and alumni can provide valuable insights and recommendations for ongoing program improvement. In addition, campus ministers can avail themselves of national survey data—available through such institutions as Georgetown's Center for

Applied Research in the Apostolate (CARA), the Pew Research Center, and UCLA's Higher Education Research Institute (HERI)—in order to compare and contrast their local college experiences, to assess current programs, to plan changes in future events, and to choose new and innovative projects to undertake.

RECOMMENDED READING

Sandra M. Estanek, Michael James, et al., have developed an excellent pamphlet summarizing key principles to guide student affairs professionals at Catholic colleges and universities: *Principles for Good Practice for Student Affairs at Catholic Colleges and Universities* (Washington, DC: Association for Student Affairs at Catholic Colleges and Universities, 2007). This document can be retrieved from the Internet at http://www.asaccu.org/images/principles%20 of%20good%20practice%202nd%20edition.pdf.

For campus ministers interested in a thorough overview of the goals and dynamics of service-learning programs, Janet Eyler and Dwight E. Giles, Jr., provide an accessible manual in *Where's the Learning in Service-Learning?* (San Francisco: Jossey-Bass, 1999).

CHAPTER SIX

STUDENT LIFE AND CAMPUS MINISTRY

ANY DISCUSSION OF STUDENT LIFE needs to consider what some common characteristics of today's students are, as well as what life is like on a campus. Clearly, no two institutions are identical. Yet a glance at some typical student comments from one institution might give us an idea of today's college scene. For instance, in considering the academic offerings, some students responded: "Global awareness programs and seminars are routine, and a strong community-service ethic permeates the atmosphere"…"Class sizes are small, and [the] academic experience [is] intimate and intellectual"…"Like at most Catholic schools, you're required to take everything from English to philosophy to religion here"…"The core curriculum is a b***h, but it does expose you to considerable wisdom."[1]

When speaking about life on the campus, other students thought that those who are administrators in housing "just put people together with no thought to whether they are compatible." They were somewhat negative about the spirit on campus when they said that "student groups consist of only the hard-cores," and that "the lack of school spirit can be quite a downer." "Drinking is prevalent," they added. Students "smoke a lot of weed," but "there isn't a big party scene other than little get-togethers in the dorms."[2]

With regard to the composition of the student body, a typical remark was: "The Asian and Latino populations are especially high, and there's a noticeable international contingent." According to many females, the ratio of women to men is "pitiful." It's "pretty hard to date or even hook up if you are straight" because "most guys are taken or gay." Some students "dress in alternative or funky clothing" and are "experimental" with everything from sexuality and music to drugs. "Many students are Catholic but aren't necessarily strictly practicing"..."A lot of people smoke cigarettes"..."There are science nerds, hippies, and the occasional shopping addict"..."Some students are outspoken and outgoing"...Others "have their iPods on *all the time*"... "People are passionate. Some are lazy. A few are beautifully artistic. A bunch are athletic. A couple are phony. Some are damn smart. Others are pretty ignorant. But at least we got it all...."[3]

Although each institution is unique, and these "evaluations" are anecdotal, such comments reflect the diversity found in the student body: students take academics to varying degrees of seriousness; they are experimenting with sex and drugs; they are irregular in their religious practices; they are tied to their cell phones and iPods; and they are concerned about dorm life. Other factors that affect almost all college students are economics (rich students and those who are on scholarship), sexual orientation, and family background. These people are a sample of those who walk through the doors of institutions of higher education. The challenge for Catholic colleges and universities is to provide for these students both academically and spiritually.

From an academic point of view, the goal is straightforward: to give students the best education possible with available resources. Through formal classes, seminars, and immersion experiences, the institution brings about a certain unity. Students take classes together, they have the same teachers, and they are part of a group undergoing immersion experiences. From a religious point of view, however, building community can be more difficult since not all students are Catholic, and the Catholics often enough do not practice their faith or know very little about it. This problem is not new. The late biblical scholar Raymond Brown commented that, in the first century, the "disturbed state of Christians at Corinth" caused St. Paul to give the people who lived there much attention. Brown went on to say:

Paradoxically, the range of their problems (rival "theologians," factions, problematic sexual practices, marital obligations, liturgy, church roles) make the correspondence exceptionally instructive for troubled Christians and churches of our times. Attempts to live according to the gospel in the multiethnic and crosscultural society at Corinth raised issues still encountered in multiethnic, multiracial, and crosscultural societies today.[4]

In dealing with college students, there are usually two offices on campus, student life and campus ministry, that impact the day-to-day events in students' lives. Both offices overlap somewhat in handling campus functions. For instance, both are interested in the living situation on campus. This implies that the institution has criteria for selecting the personnel who oversee life in the resident halls and living quarters. This selection process usually considers at least three aspects: (1) the persons who choose the personnel who oversee and live with the students; (2) the norms used in making the selection; and, (3) in a Catholic institution, the religious values the institution wishes to stress. Input from campus ministry should be especially considered in this third point. In many cases, staff people from campus ministry live in the residence halls. The people who work in the residence halls usually have a strong influence on students, and have an excellent opportunity to convey a value system and the school's mission and vision. Because of this, dialogue between campus ministry and student life is essential regarding where people live during their college years.

Historically, most college service programs first began in campus ministry. From there they spread to other areas of the institution, including the office of student life. Service programs developed into immersion programs. Immersion experiences soon went beyond the campus and involved travel to both domestic and foreign sites. Obviously, the office of student life sponsors many of these projects. This is yet another area where close collaboration between the office of student life and campus ministry is extremely important. Previously, we had mentioned how campus ministry can provide a spiritual presence as well as faith reflection for these projects so that the experiences are seen in relationship to the mission, goals, and Catholic identity of the institution. But, in fact, only in a few Catholic institutions does the campus ministry office administer the majority of service programs. This situation has provoked a common criticism that many Catholic colleges seriously lack faith-influenced programs.

This chapter will focus on the uniqueness of campus ministry's contribution to a college or university (as opposed to the contribution of the office of student life). Six areas immediately come to mind: (1) providing religious counseling; (2) fostering sensitivity to the diversity of faiths of the students and faculty; (3) developing and deepening individuals' faith; (4) providing religious services (liturgies and retreats); (5) examining issues from the dimensions of faith and social justice; (6) being an intellectual stimulus outside the classroom. Obviously, members of the campus ministry team should be able to deal with these areas if they are to be effective. Let us comment on each of these areas.

Counseling takes on many forms. Most academic institutions have a professional counseling center. However, much informal counseling takes place in interaction between students and those in the student life offices, people living in the residence halls, and so on. Often enough, students (and sometimes faculty) have questions with regard to religious issues. This latter area is where campus ministry plays a role, though its staff members are also involved at other levels. Sometimes questions arise regarding faith itself, Church teachings and practices, and the relevance of organized religion. Typical issues might include the morality of buying products from companies whose employees live in almost slave conditions, attitudes toward ROTC and war, and even concerns over bankruptcy. Such a variety of questions implies that members of the campus ministry staff need good academic training so that they can relate to the student and faculty concerns, as well as be aware of the issues of the day.

Counseling, especially pastoral counseling, is one reason why people seek out campus ministry. People want spiritual or religious input with regard to some aspect of their lives. Students frequently enough wish to have a "safe place" where their values are reinforced and where they have the opportunity to talk to people who share and are committed to their own faith. Sometimes this input can be done on a group level. For those wishing to know about becoming Catholics or wanting to know more about their faith, campus ministry can provide programs for those who share this common interest. Others might be interested in marriage preparation. Again, much of this can be accomplished with several people together. A group approach is definitely preferable when people desire mutual support. More frequently, however, people want to talk to someone on a one-on-one basis about something personal. Discussion in areas of faith and morality are common. The topics are endless, however, and can be as diverse as a person's relationship with his or her own family, use of drugs, cohabitation, failing grades, loneliness, the relevance of organized religion, thoughts of suicide, and so on. Those on the team need to ask themselves: "Is this something I can handle, or should I refer the person to someone else more qualified?"

Often enough, for the first time in their lives, students living in a residence hall have roommates who are members of a different faith (if they profess a faith at all), or who are of another ethnic group, or who have a different sexual orientation. The anecdotal remarks about housing at the beginning of this chapter reflect these concerns. Obviously these are situations that student life must address. Yet campus ministry, the counseling center, and other areas of the institution are also involved. Campus ministry is challenged to provide an ecumenical atmosphere so that others' religious beliefs are respected and their positive values are accentuated. Obviously, campus ministry then needs to address the social and moral issues that arise from such a diversity of backgrounds. An ecumenical approach is necessary in today's world.

Sometimes Catholics are afraid of ecumenism and see it as a threat to their faith. However, today most Catholic institutions of higher education offer courses on crosscultural ethics, sponsor interfaith prayer services, and maintain an academic interest in what others believe. During the last half century, Catholics have realized that they do not possess all knowledge: God can and does act through other faiths, both Christian and non-Christian.[5] Campus ministry has many opportunities to foster dialogue and respect between Catholics and those who do not share Catholic beliefs.

An excellent example of such an ecumenical pastoral approach can be seen in a speech in Casablanca that Pope John Paul II gave to over 100,000 young Muslims in 1985. King Hassan II of Morocco had invited the pope to give this talk. We can imagine the scene of an aging European Catholic speaking to young North African Muslims. In this particular talk, the pope spoke about God inviting change and belief. Some themes that the pope highlighted were a common witness to the meaning of God and human dignity, the responsibility of the young to make the world more humane and pluralistic, and the necessity of seeking suitable working conditions for all. He reminded the young people of the value of study, encouraged them to grow in their spiritual life, and ended with a prayer that God would continue to fill them with gifts.[6]

What specifically should a college or university expect campus ministry to provide? A good place to begin is to examine the challenge to help students, faculty, and staff develop and possess a mature faith. Obviously, this approach avoids the two extremes of fundamentalism and the attitude of "everything goes." The approach must appeal to the intellectual as well as to the religious and social dimensions of people. Thus, campus ministry needs to motivate students to not be content with the status quo, but to reach beyond their own comfortable surroundings. In positive terms, campus ministry should be the strong religious partner in promoting the full human development of students, faculty, administrators, and staff in the community. How is this done?

When people hear the term *campus ministry*, most think of liturgy. For Catholics this means providing Masses; for non-Catholics this suggests putting people in touch with their faith tradition on a regular basis. The liturgy can and should be adapted to the people who are participating in it.

Catholic Colleges in the 21st Century

At a college or university, the congregation consists of students and those connected with the institution. This enables campus ministry to focus on a particular target group. Saturday and Sunday liturgies provide a unique weekly opportunity to help people integrate their tradition with their current life situations. The greater the participation of the people present, the more effective will be the liturgy. Some Catholic institutions sponsor "residence hall Masses," where smaller groups meet on a weeknight on a more informal basis. Those present in the smaller groups are more likely to become personally involved in the liturgy than they would in a larger setting. Likewise, when campus ministry recommends to non-Catholics places to worship, the staff usually highlights sites nearby where college students will feel at home, and the services appeal to that mentality and age group.

Retreats have always been a tradition at Catholic institutions of higher education. In past years, mandatory retreats were "preached" by a priest to a large audience, but with very little interaction with the group. Today, at most Catholic colleges, retreats are still very much a part of the scene, but usually several small retreats during the year now take the place of the traditional large retreat held at the beginning of the academic year. These small retreats are not mandatory and usually have a varied format. The advantage of such an approach is that people are present because they want to be present. For some participants, the big revelation is that they can live for a day without a cell phone or computer.

A retreat experience enables people to spend time contemplating their relationship to God and to their neighbor, as well as their beliefs in the current context. Obviously the formats will vary from institution to institution (and within an institution), because of the different compositions of student bodies. As we mentioned, popular retreat formats include those from Kairos and the CYO. Both of these involve students working with students as peer ministers or mentors. This method is usually more effective than having an older person telling the younger ones what to do. Since a retreat in such a format is not held in a big chapel, people usually go some place away from campus, or stay out of the mainstream of the campus for a day or so. This type of retreat entails costs, so campus ministry needs to provide sufficient funds for those who cannot pay. Obviously, this should be a consideration when the institution draws up its annual budget.

The proliferation of immersion programs challenges the campus ministry team to provide a social justice and faith dimension to these experiences. The question is how. Can the team be involved in every single immersion program offered on campus? Does that involvement mean that someone on the team is tied up for a period and cannot work on something else? Much depends on the institutional values, as well as funding and staffing. If an institution sees the importance of challenging students to think critically about the faith dimension of their lives, that institution will give tangible financial and human resource support. Members of the campus ministry team will also need to be creative in their use of time and resources. If the institution does not provide the capital support, then campus ministry will need to rethink its goals and prioritize them. Immersion programs of themselves do not necessarily imply faith and justice dimensions.

A current phenomenon on campuses today is that of discussion groups, both formal and informal. Many of these are led by non-Catholic students who are interested in religion. A popular topic is the Bible. Usually some form of fellowship accompanies these discussions. An advantage of a discussion group is that it involves peers talking among and with each other. Like the Kairos retreat format, this "horizontal" approach (student to student) is usually more effective than the "vertical" one (teacher to student).

Obviously, topics that center on moral and political issues generate much interest. The daily news usually stresses the close connections between politics and religion in many parts of the world. Catholic social teaching is concerned with areas of science, economics, sexuality, migrants, underdeveloped nations, and refugees. Today, cultural pluralism is a fact of life on campuses, same sex marriage is debated, and the role of war is an especially sensitive issue to those who are being recruited to serve in the armed forces. Discussion groups provide a useful forum to air opinions on such controversial topics. Since these themes are connected to religious practice, they give campus ministry an opportunity to offer a Catholic presence in the discussions.

The demographics of today's Church show that future leadership will be found among the laity. This situation recalls the very early Church before clergy came into existence. The lay movement was as successful then as it is today among many faith communities. "The University is where the Church does its thinking,"[7] said the longtime president of the University of Notre Dame, Father Theodore Hesburgh. Institutions of higher education are in a position to influence future directions of the Church. Campus ministry has a unique position of being able to apply academic concepts to the practical—meaning, pastoral—aspects of daily life. This is indeed an appropriate preparation for future leaders in the Church. These future leaders will have experienced the theoretical and practical realities of today's world as well as their pastoral and moral implications for the Church of the future. These leaders of tomorrow should be able to use their insights to help the next generations. Campus ministry needs to be a place where persons of all faiths can ask questions about the Catholic tradition and feel welcome when they do so.

We have highlighted some common areas that campus ministry shares with other offices and departments within a college or university. This list is certainly not exhaustive. However, in each area campus ministry has something unique to contribute to the common good amid so much diversity. The overall aim is to build community in such an environment where diversity can actually strengthen the unity of the college or university. Good and bad aspects are found in the history of campus ministry. In some places, campus ministers have had no job description other than to do what the president has told them to do. That frequently involves picking up temporary tasks that no one else wants. This lack of job description can be beneficial if the director has vision and the ability to set the agenda (and sufficient money). That combination is rare, however. Over the years, other departments have taken over some of the traditional roles played by campus ministry. Yet the six goals mentioned above can and have been attained.

To mention a success story, Boston College provides a good model of what can be done. Like most other Catholic colleges, BC has many students who are frequently secular themselves and sometimes are not even culturally Catholic. The administration realizes that persons who oversee immersion experiences often possess the faith themselves, but do not know how to help students make the connection between the experience and faith. Therefore, the majority of that institution's service programs are run out of campus ministry (as opposed to the student/university life office) to ensure the faith dimension.

What qualities should colleges and universities look for when they hire personnel to form the campus ministry team? Let us begin with the director. Since the director is the leader of the team, he or she must have administrative skills, and be able to work effectively with members of the team as well as with the various officers of the institution. Given the importance and nature of the job, the director should be a member of the president's cabinet (or similar position). He or she should have at least a master's degree in theology (or pastoral ministry) and at least five years of pastoral experience. Three of those five years should be in a campus ministry position, either at a college or university, or a similar position at a high school or parish. In recruiting members of the team, the director must keep in mind a balance of gender, ethnicity, and age.

Not only the director, but also each member of the campus ministry team should have a master's degree in either theology or pastoral ministry. Like the director, they should have some previous experience in a campus ministry environment. That could be as an intern in campus ministry, or in similar work in a parish or high school. Since, by definition, we are talking about a Catholic institution, a Catholic member of the team is usually preferred. The diversity of the student body, however, usually requires that one or more competent persons of another faith be hired as part of the team. In any case, the person should possess a mature faith, have a balanced personality, and be committed to the institution's mission and vision.

Members of the team can "specialize" in some aspect or another, but, in general, the whole team needs to respond to the many and varied demands. These demands range from responding to simple questions to providing grief counseling (such as helping people face the death of a parent or close friend), to supporting a student who is breaking up a relationship. Because campus ministry is identified with a pastoral approach, members of the team should be able to effectively lead groups in prayer, liturgies, and retreats. Obviously, to interact successfully the team members need to have personalities that attract people.

In his 1961 inaugural address, President Kennedy challenged people: "Ask not what your country can do for you—ask what you can do for your country." Yet now, fifty years later, people's interests center around *I* and *me* rather than *we* and *us*. The common good and social justice concerns seem to have been forgotten during the last half century. Fortunately, globalization has forced us to realize that a more equitable sharing of the world's limited resources is necessary, and that, as people of faith, we need to think of our neighbor in whatever we do. This sociopolitical context provides campus ministry with a wonderful opportunity to address the relationship between faith and social justice in very practical terms.

The preceding paragraphs give us examples of the many, varied roles that campus ministry plays in Catholic institutions of higher education. Usually much less homogeneity exists at this level than in secondary schools, where the composition of the student body is more uniform and the class offerings are less diverse. Yet both share in three common areas of concern: funding, updating, and evaluation. Let us take these three individually.

Funding will depend on the value the institution puts on the importance of the role of campus ministry. Frequently a discrepancy exists between the institution's rhetoric and the facts. The pie chart we mentioned in chapter 1 gives us a graphic example. When the institution makes up its yearly budget, how big are the slices allotted to various programs such as campus ministry? If an institution boasts about its faith commitment but does not allot sufficient funds to implement that commitment, a question arises as to the credibility of its claims. In making up the budget, the institution also needs to look at the pay scale for members of the team. Are their salaries equal to or even above those who hold comparable jobs (e.g., in the student life office)? Does the institution make allowance for the irregular schedules that members of the team must follow? Is the institution willing to support a staff that is big enough to implement its mission and vision? How well are campus ministry projects funded (such as providing retreat experiences)? In its capital campaigns, has the institution highlighted the role of campus ministry, as well as urged donors to pledge funds to that specific office? Does the development or advancement office advertise campus ministry? Do capital-campaign brochures publicize the institution's Catholic identity and its implementation by campus ministry? These questions regarding funding help people evaluate concretely how seriously the institution takes the role of and office of campus ministry. One way by which we can examine the importance that an institution gives to campus ministry is to compare its funding to that of other Catholic institutions of higher education that have a comparable number of students.

Colleges and universities encourage their faculty members to stay updated in their fields. To promote and facilitate this, colleges offer sabbatical years and raises in rank and pay. People on the faculty are usually evaluated on a regular basis. The principle is to keep up with developments in one's field. Likewise, those who serve on the campus ministry team need periodic evaluation and updating. This can take the form of attending workshops and conferences that are relevant to one's particular interest and the institution's needs, enrolling in professional development courses, and doing reading in the field. Some of these projects need funding. Others might just involve allowing people some time off to better themselves. In any case, the institution needs to promote a truly professional staff.

Almost every group has some type of evaluation of its program and outcomes. This type of assessment provides information about how effective that group is, whether it has fulfilled its objectives and goals, what can be improved, what is lacking, and other specific information. Assessment is something that Father Nicolás mentioned as necessary (as we quoted him in chapter 4). Certainly, evaluations are something that also needs to be carried out with campus ministry. Not only members of the team but also the whole program needs to be scrutinized on a regular basis. What was appropriate for and what impacted many people five years ago might be obsolete now. New structures and a new focus might be needed. At times, the results of an evaluation might come as a shock, but if they take place on a regular basis, the necessary changes can sometimes be relatively painless. Campus ministry's office and team should be treated as professionals. This practice is very much in keeping with Scripture that says, "From everyone to whom much has been given, much will be required; and from the one to whom much has been entrusted, even more will be demanded" (Luke 12:48).

RECOMMENDED READING

Psychological counseling and religious counseling are compared and contrasted in Rodger Bufford's chapter entitled "Consecrated Counseling: Reflections on the Distinctives of Christian Counseling," in *Psychology and Christianity Integration: Seminal Works That Shaped the Movement*, Daryl H. Stevenson, Brian E. Eck, and Peter C. Hill, eds. (Batavia, IL: Christian Association for Psychological Studies, 2007), 253–63.

Donald Shockley gives an overview of the history, theology, and mission of campus ministry in his book *Campus Ministry: The Church beyond Itself* (Louisville, KY: Westminster/John Knox Press, 1989).

The Catholic Campus Ministry Association spells out the certification requirements for its members at http://www.ccmanet.org/ccma. nsf/certification?OpenPage. Most of these recommendations have been covered in this chapter.

CHAPTER SEVEN

SOCIAL AND POLITICAL ENGAGEMENT

IN THE LAST CHAPTER we saw how the realities of student life have altered the direction of campus ministry. Within the context of the twentieth and twenty-first centuries, new social and political concerns have arisen that frame the way in which campus ministry teams approach their work on Catholic college campuses. Let us now look at some of these profound shifts from a social and political perspective. In light of these dramatic changes in values and vision at Catholic colleges and universities, we can more clearly discern the direction that campus ministry should take in the twenty-first century.

In 1973, on July 31, the feast of St. Ignatius, Father Pedro Arrupe, SJ, first used the term *men and women for others*. Then superior general of the Jesuits, Father Arrupe was addressing the Tenth International Congress of Jesuit Alumni of Europe. In coining this term, he began a process for the Society of Jesus, and indirectly for many other religious congregations, of reviewing the core values and mission of Catholic schools and colleges:

> Today our prime educational objective must be to form men [and women] for others; men [and women] who will live not for themselves but for God and his Christ—for the God-man who lived and died for all the world; men [and women] who cannot even conceive of love of God which does not include love for the least of their neighbors; men

77

[and women] completely convinced that love of God which does not issue in justice for others is a farce.[1]

In essence, by giving this address, Arrupe changed the focus of Jesuit as well as all Catholic education to embrace social justice. Many other religious congregations and dioceses have espoused similar core values for their institutions of higher education. Two typical examples of this trend to integrate education and social justice are given by the priests and brothers of the Congregation of the Holy Cross and the priests and brothers of the Society of Mary (Marianists). The University of Portland and the University of Notre Dame were established by the Congregation of the Holy Cross, whose founder was Blessed Fr. Basil Moreau, CSC. In 1849, Father Moreau stated: "An education that is complete is one in which the hands and heart are engaged as much as the mind. We want to let our students try their learning in the world and so make prayers of their educations."[2] The University of Dayton, St. Mary's University in San Antonio, and Chaminade University of Honolulu were founded by the Marianists, whose mission statement also clearly articulates the integration of education and social justice:

> Wherever we are sent we invite others to share in Mary's mission of making Christ present in every age and culture by forming persons and communities of apostolic faith that advance justice and reconciliation. Committed to education, we minister with youth and in solidarity with the poor.[3]

Not unlike past generations, today's college students on Catholic campuses have concerns and interests that reflect the signs of the times and the contexts in which they live. One of these concerns directly relates to the role of campus ministry in the twenty-first century: the integration of their faith or religious tradition with their personal identity as emerging adults. Along with this challenge, questions or doubts about personal identity and self-confidence surface. These uncertainties play into the unique life task of the Millennials (Gen Y-ers) in emerging from adolescence into full adulthood. For many, this process takes place during their years at a college or university, although it often continues for several years thereafter.

Campus ministry teams have the responsibility to serve as guides to assist these emerging adults to sort out a number of often-conflicting values: pressures from their peers immersed in the hook-up culture, as well as demands generated by a hyper-commercialized, technocratic society that associates meaning and self-worth with the latest and trendiest products. Just how do college students sift through these apparent "affective landmines"? One answer is to turn to prayer, reflection, and quiet, all of which require time, dedication, and consistency. In our postmodern culture, which is tremendously driven by career choice and a market-based economy, emerging adults at U.S. Catholic colleges need the aid of campus ministers—and of other professionals, for that matter—to provide the appropriate training, direction, and opportunities so that they can explore these new methods of self-integration and discernment. Catholic institutions of higher education with clearly articulated core values, as well as mission and identity statements, provide the best locus for all of this nurturing to take place.

Of course, as we have already seen earlier, one obvious issue for campus ministry teams to confront is the trend among college students to differentiate spirituality from institutionalized religion. Since spirituality tends to be popularly perceived as individual rather communal, this trend presents particular difficulties when campus ministry strives to promote organized communal liturgies, retreats, and other prayer experiences. Essential to a successful approach will be working with groups of college students who are already invested in the communal nature of their faith. These student leaders will be instrumental in inviting, encouraging, and even challenging their peers to participate in faith-formation gatherings of any type.

One unique approach for campus ministers to consider in dealing with the current Millennial dilemma is guidance in vocational discernment. Although the career services office provides excellent opportunities to counsel students about their career options, as well as train them in the interviewing process for employment, Catholic colleges and universities have the additional responsibility of providing spiritual and pastoral guidance concerning vocation decisions. Here the student's spirituality and real life intersect in a unique way. Campus ministers are the most indicated to provide individual and collective faith reflection on how God is calling all students to particular vocations in their life in community.[4] Regardless of their religious affiliation, students on Catholic college campuses should be challenged to reflect deeply on how they can best use their talents and gifts for the service of faith and the promotion of justice in our global community. Both personal and communal, this call to discernment obligates students in Catholic institutions of higher education to pose those deeper questions about their life goals that entail vocational decision making: whether to commit one's life as a married person, single person, clergyperson, or religious brother or sister as the means to best serve the family of humankind. Campus ministry teams should strategize how they can best meet this need for discernment in their particular campus context.

At least three events in the last fifty years have influenced the direction that Catholic colleges have taken with regard to the way they present their curricula in general, and their religious aspects in particular. The first event was Vatican II, the second was a United States Supreme Court decision, and the third was the Thirty-second General Congregation of Jesuits. These three milestones (and we do not limit our comments to them) caused a ripple effect on Catholic education that began in the 1960s and continues today. Let us say something about each one of them.

As we previously mentioned, Vatican II (1962–65) specifically addressed "The Church in the Modern World." That document spoke of the "griefs and anxieties" of this age and stated that its message was addressed "to the whole of humanity."[5] Not only did all sixteen documents of the Council root the Church in history, but this particular one spoke of the changed conditions in which people found themselves, especially in regard to scientific advances. This document also critiqued those who think that "religion consists in acts of worship alone and in the discharge of certain moral obligations," and asserted that the "split between the faith which many profess and their daily lives deserves to be counted among the more serious errors of our age."[6]

While Vatican II was in session, the United States Supreme Court handed down a decision that would directly affect colleges and universities, and upgrade the role of "religious studies" in public school curriculum. This ruling would also indirectly affect private institutions. In 1963, the Court stated:

> It might well be said that one's education is not complete without a study of comparative religion or the history of religion and its relationship to the advancement of civilization. It certainly may be said that the Bible is worthy of study for its literary and historic qualities. Nothing we have said here indicates that such study of the Bible or of religion, when presented objectively as part of a secular program of education, may not be effected consistently with the First Amendment.[7]

With this decision, the number of religious studies courses in public colleges proliferated. The academic study of religion had now become respectable at these institutions. At the same time, the individual states were founding numerous "community colleges." This caused many Catholic colleges and universities to rethink their programs and to ask themselves: "How are we different? State schools now offer religious studies courses for credit. Why should we even have a Catholic college?"

The response to their questions was articulated a few years later in 1975. At that time, the Jesuit order affirmed the link between belief and practice when it said: "Christian salvation consists in an undivided love of the Father and of the neighbor and of justice. Since evangelization is proclamation of that faith which is made operative in love of others, the promotion of justice is indispensable to it."[8] Thus, the Jesuits formally linked theory to practice. This official statement of the Jesuit order followed up the 1973 address of Father Arrupe that we cited earlier in this chapter.

At the same time, schools of divinity had begun to offer a new degree, the master of divinity. The purpose of this particular degree was to help those who were preparing for the priesthood and ministry to apply their learning directly to pastoral situations, rather than studying in isolation. For example, part of the curriculum was devoted to preaching (making the Bible relevant to the audience), hospital work (dealing with the sick), and applying moral theory to concrete issues. The word *practicum* became a more common part of academic vocabulary. Meanwhile the Vietnam War was bringing up concerns such as conscientious objection to serving in the military, the role of ROTC on college campuses, and the problems of racial equality—that is, whether the burden of serving in the military fell more on one group than another. Religions needed to involve themselves in these issues. The influence and methods of the practical master of divinity degree became increasingly important on Catholic campuses, as they needed to respond to questions raised by current developments.

Campus ministry arose in this atmosphere. As we saw in chapter 1, no longer were the Sodality and the Knights of Columbus, or even the college chaplain's office, considered sufficient to complement classroom teaching. Both faculty and students needed to confront the dynamic contemporary world. Religious practices that ignored history were becoming increasingly irrelevant. In Catholic institutions, the faith perspective was considered an essential part of people's liberal education. Clearly, some people could object: what connection does religion have with chemistry or physics? Such a question implies considering such a discipline in isolation, yet how we apply chemistry and physics *does* raise moral questions. For example, during the Vietnam War, the

Dow Chemical Company was producing napalm and Agent Orange, which the U.S. armed forces then used to maim and kill innocent people. This use of chemistry was not an isolated theoretical problem. It prompted massive negative reactions from people, especially college students. Likewise, those who chose to major in business became aware that the moral code of many companies was reduced to "enlightened self-interest." We might then ask ourselves, "What are some current concerns?"

Today people are realizing that pollution involves more than troops on the battlefield and innocent civilians. The whole future of the planet is at stake. Ecology takes many forms as humanity fulfills its purpose to take care of God's creation: "to till it and keep it" (Gen 2:15); and, "the earth is the Lord's and all that is in it" (Ps 24:1). Campus ministry has usually taken the lead in making people aware of such concerns, by sponsoring study groups and providing panel discussions and workshops that examine these issues from a faith perspective. This process heightens group awareness, resulting in people from various areas in the institution coming to the realization that a direct connection exists between what people believe and how they should act, as *Gaudium et Spes* indicated. Even St. Paul attributed damage to the planet as a result of human sinfulness (Rom 8:20–21).

Campus ministry in Catholic institutions does not limit itself to the physical effects of the problems studied in ecology; it also challenges people to consider religious perspectives when they inform their consciences. Obviously, campus ministry must do this in the context of the given institution, its history, and its curriculum. However, since life in general has become more specialized and complex, campus ministry cannot do this task alone. Catholic colleges and universities, under the encouragement of campus ministry teams, need to raise concerns about many other current issues, such as homelessness, rent control, fair housing, comprehensive and affordable medical care, and hunger. To address these concerns effectively, the office of campus ministry must team up with other departments of their institution. One exam-

83

ple would be tapping the intellectual training of the political science department by partnering up to develop and promote effective service-learning projects in the areas just mentioned. Students could be given academic credit for taking part in supervised activities. Because each institution is unique, there is no "one size fits all" approach.

While we have highlighted campus ministry's involvement with the social and religious issues that students and faculty face at Catholic institutions of higher education, we should not neglect the importance of the "traditional" work also done by campus ministry. This includes providing liturgies adapted to the college congregation, retreats and days of recollection, marriage preparation, and pastoral counseling. As we pointed out previously in citing Vatican II's stance toward the modern world, all these activities should be integrated into the daily lives of students and faculty members and not compartmentalized.

One word that probably best summarizes the role of campus ministry is *community*. A community has certain goals. Its membership changes over the years, yet continuity exists from its beginnings. If a community is to survive, it must always adapt to its environment. Stagnation means death in some form.

We often speak of the "university community" or a "community of scholars and learners," and so on. For Catholic institutions of higher education, campus ministry should provide practical (pastoral) opportunities for members of that community to integrate their religious experiences with the intellectual and the social aspects of their lives. They need to do this in companionship with others in the context of the time and place in which they live.

In 1624, John Donne wrote that, since the Church is universal, so are her actions. When she baptizes a child, that child is grafted into the body of the Church of which we too are members. The same reasoning holds when we bury a person. That concerns us. Our lives are chapters in a book that has many translators. The chapters are not torn out of the book, and God's hand is in every translation. Donne then added his famous line that "no man is an island." He developed the theme that when someone dies and we hear the bell, it tolls for us. We are all part of the human community.[9]

Donne's thoughts apply to the role of campus ministry in developing community. Members of that holistic community realize that their gifts are to be shared, and that each one profits from the love, friendship, and talents of others. The religious dimension, both theoretical and practical, is an important part of higher education at Catholic institutions. Campus ministry with its multifaceted approach has an important and unique role to play in the "Catholicity" of the institution. Ultimately the financial and moral support given by the institution sends a clear message to all about the value administrators place on the Catholic identity of the institution.

RECOMMENDED READING

For a thorough analysis of the context of adult Catholics and their faith in the contemporary United States, see Tim Muldoon's *Seeds of Hope: Young Adults and the Catholic Church in the United States* (Mahwah, NJ: Paulist Press, 2007).

To learn more about the rise in Catholic college students' interest in traditional values and practice, see Naomi Schaefer Riley's *God on the Quad: How Religious Colleges and the Missionary Generation Are Changing America* (New York: St. Martin's Press, 2005).

Sociologist Robert Wuthnow reports on research of young adults' practice of religion, their experience of spirituality, emerging trends, and the effect all of these can have on the future of churches, in *After the Baby Boomers: How Twenty- and Thirty-Somethings Are Shaping the Future of American Religion* (Princeton, NJ: Princeton University Press, 2007).

CHAPTER EIGHT

THE EMERGENT CHURCH OF THE TWENTY-FIRST CENTURY

IN HIS OPENING SPEECH AT the Second Vatican Council, Pope John XXIII spoke of the "prophets of gloom, who are always forecasting disaster, as though the end of the world were at hand." He disagreed with such people and took a much more positive approach: "In the present order of things," he said, "Divine Providence is leading us to a new order of human relation which, by men's [and women's] own efforts and even beyond their very expectations, are directed toward the fulfillment of God's superior and inscrutable designs. And everything, even human differences, leads to the greater good of the Church."[1]

As we look back at the Second Vatican Council, we see that its documents take a positive rather than a negative approach to the world. In many respects, this is a reversal of the attitude of the previous four hundred years, during which Catholics seemed to define themselves by what they were not and by what they refused to accept. Quite notably in contrast, the Council's document *Gaudium et Spes* ("The Church in the Modern World") begins with the words *joy and hope.*

In chapter 1 we looked at the changes that have taken place on colleges campuses after Vatican II ended, while in chapter 2 we examined the profile of students on Catholic college campuses today. The extremely diverse world that students encounter today reminds us of similar situations in the very early Church, especially in big cities like Corinth, Athens, and Antioch. In those chapters, we discussed notable changes in Catholic higher education: a vast majority of the institutions have diminished the number of philosophy and theology requirements. Not only do many students who are not Catholic now attend these institutions, but so do those who self-identify as Catholic but frequently know little about their faith. Fortunately, most schools today do not take a "one size fits all" approach. Immersion experiences, various types of retreats, and ecumenical dialogue are all part of the scene on most campuses. A pluralism of thought and experience predominates. Yet some people are very vocal in their opposition to such changes. Since Vatican II, a number of conservative Catholic colleges have arisen that oppose anything that is not "traditional." Organizations like the Cardinal Newman Society find these trends alarming.

In contrast, we found highly motivated students working on service projects, volunteering their time to work for nonprofit organizations, with still others devoting a year or two after their graduation to work in the inner city or in a Third World country. They see value in direct service to their neighbor. Some colleges have requirements that include diversity studies and similar experiences if the student is to receive an undergraduate degree.

We also saw in chapter 2 the disconnect that frequently exists between organized religion and personal spirituality. This is especially evident in the area of sexuality. Many people consider themselves Catholic, but yet do not accept or practice the Church's official teaching in this area. Others consider themselves to be "spiritual," but refuse to become part of any organized religion. By doing so, they set their own norms and are not challenged by others. This can be viewed as an extension of traditional American rugged individualism. Such people are not interested in living according to any religious community norms. They do not wish to define themselves by relationships.

Any institution that calls itself Catholic should ultimately relate itself to Jesus Christ. The movement that he started nearly 2,000 years ago continues in that organization which today we call the Church. Although the Church is multicultural (and has been for most of its existence), the initial group was Jewish. The earliest writings of the New Testament, the letters of St. Paul, describe some of the problems involved when others who were not Jewish joined the movement. These "outsiders" realized that Jesus' message was not confined to a certain ethnic group or a certain part of the known world. The movement inspired by Jesus suffered "growing pains" and persecution, similar to those that Jesus himself faced. Very early on, the people who belonged to this movement were called Christians (Acts 11:26), thus being identified as those who followed the teachings of Jesus Christ. One of the best known of the early communities was located at Antioch, at that time the third largest city in the Roman Empire. It was populated by both Jews and Gentiles.

The early Christian community was of "one heart and soul." As an emergent Church, its members held their material goods in common so that "there was not a needy person among them, for as many as owned lands or houses sold them and brought the proceeds of what was sold…and laid it at the apostles' feet, and it was distributed to each as any had need" (Acts 4:32–35). St. Paul compared the early communities to a body that has many members. He stressed that all had different gifts (for example, teaching, leading, and ministering) but all are part of the same body (Rom 12:4–8). The idea of social justice practiced by community members has its roots all the way back to the Old Testament, and was vividly expressed by Jesus in examples such as the parables of the Good Samaritan (Luke 10:30–37) and the final judgment (Matt 25:31–46). In these narratives, Jesus spoke of doing good works for fellow humans, even non-Jews. During his public life, Jesus sent his close followers on a "missionary experiment" that was modeled on his own ministry (Matt 10:5–16). Thus, the Jesus movement practiced social justice from its very onset, and adapted to the local situation.

At the beginning of his epistles, St. Paul referred to members of the Jesus movement who gathered in specific localities as the churches. In the First Epistle to the Corinthians, he tells the members of that "church" that they are "the body of Christ." This expression refers both to the local community (1 Cor 12:13) and to the Eucharist (1 Cor 11:23–27). When we read these passages, which are placed close together in the same letter, we realize that the community should celebrate the Lord's Supper by meeting together regularly, and sharing the same bread and same cup. In fact, Paul became so upset with the lack of mutual respect that he needed to remind his readers that when they "come together to eat," they should "wait for one another." He did not wish some people to leave early after having eaten all the good food, but wanted some type of equality to exist (something that he expressed in Gal 3:27–28).

Even though St. Paul does not mention much about church structure and organization in his main letters, the Pastoral Epistles do speak of various "offices," such as those of "bishop" and "deacon." With the introduction of these "offices," a structure of the early community began to develop. The purpose of this structure was to facilitate the continuation of the mission of Jesus in the growing, emerging Church.

Over the centuries, the structure became increasingly more complex. This leads us to question: What is the relationship between the mission itself and how the mission is carried out through these offices that represent the Church? Jon Sobrino maintains that the Church's reality lies not in itself but in a mission it is to accomplish. He adds that the Church "does not keep itself in existence through history by maintaining its structures but by constantly carrying out its mission."[2] Similarly, Jürgen Moltmann believes that it is not so much that the Church has a mission, but that the "mission of Christ creates its own church. Mission does not come from the church; it is from mission and in the light of mission that the church has to be understood."[3]

The early Church adapted itself to the different needs of the people. For instance, Acts 17:22–34 shows us some of the techniques that St. Paul used in his appeal to the Athenians, while Philip successfully converted the Ethiopian eunuch by using another approach (Acts 8:26–40). Christianity very successfully presented the message of Jesus, and by the fourth century, it became the official religion of the Roman

Empire. Yet problems were beginning to develop with having an official clergy oversee the implementation of the mission. Clergy were also interested in being financially supported, as well as interpreting the Church's mission.

Historically, tension has always existed between the mission and its maintenance. Probably the most dramatic confrontation between the two was the sixteenth-century Protestant Reformation. Although many factors such as culture and politics were involved, Church structure and the authority of the Bible were the main theological focus of the debate. The results of the split could be summarized by saying that the Catholic Church became progressively more centralized, while the Protestants became increasingly less centralized and began to split into smaller groups. Both groups were interested in educating future generations, so both founded schools at various levels. In this way, both were able to pass on their religious views while providing an education in other subjects.

At the college level in Catholic education, courses in theology and philosophy had a very prominent place in the curriculum. Sometimes Catholic and Protestant institutions considered their primary role that of proselytizing or catechizing rather than providing a well-rounded education. In the nineteenth and twentieth centuries, Catholic educational institutions in the United States were very much under the control of the local bishop. This was in part due to financial reasons: buildings and real estate were used as collateral so that the bishops could borrow money to build up their growing dioceses. Since religious sisters, brothers, and priests usually staffed the institutions, their superiors added another layer of supervision. New and creative thought in theological matters gradually became almost nonexistent in the United States. After the biggest and costliest war in history ended in the middle of the twentieth century, people had the time and the resources to reexamine and sometimes change their lifestyles. This shift in thinking became very evident at the beginning of the 1960s.

In his inaugural address of January 20, 1961, President John Kennedy said: "Let the word go forth from this time and place, to friend and foe alike, that the torch has been passed to a new generation of Americans—born in this century."[4] Change was in the air! At the same time, Catholics throughout the world were preparing the working documents for the Second Vatican Council, which would begin the following year. The Vietnam War caused people to rethink war in general. People began to question how a war in Vietnam was justified, and young people everywhere distrusted authority. Many people lost confidence in their governments—an attitude which in turn spread to Church leadership. This descriptive sweep of events of the early 1960s provides a quick glimpse of just what the Church was facing a half century ago.

Pope John XXIII was interested in taking a historical (as opposed to dogmatic) approach to theology. He wanted to make Church teaching relevant to people of the twentieth (and even the twenty-first) century. Following his lead, those who participated in Vatican II began their research by going back to original or primary sources to find out what the very early Church believed and how it approached various situations. The sixteen documents produced over the four years of the Council reflected both the historical background of the Church and how those who attended the Council thought the Church should present its teaching to the contemporary world. The immediate differences that people noticed were changing the use of Latin in the liturgy to contemporary, vernacular languages, and placing a stronger emphasis on the role of Scripture in the lives of Catholics.

How did these events affect Catholic institutions of higher education? At that time Catholic colleges and universities, like their public counterparts, had student sit-ins and protests on a variety of issues, which included revising the curriculum. Religious communities, which had been closely identified with given institutions, began to incorporate themselves legally as separate entities. No longer did religious superiors have direct control over the institutions. Catholic colleges realized that, if they were to have credibility, they must take the accrediting agencies seriously. Accreditation results were made public, and future students and their families would use them in choosing colleges.

In most places, the number of required theology courses was reduced in the curriculum revisions.

Although bishops and religious superiors no longer had direct control over most colleges and universities, some still tried to influence policy decisions. The most famous recent example was the case of the American bishops in 2009 trying to force the University of Notre Dame to "disinvite" President Obama as the commencement speaker. Forty years had elapsed since the Second Vatican Council, yet some still failed to realize that the university is the place "where the Church does its thinking," and that Catholicism had matured during the previous generation. To some, this may sound similar to parents who do not want their children to grow up, a tension that many college-age students face.

No matter how much parents fight to keep their children from encountering the realities of life, they are still humans who as social beings interact on many levels. In the era following Vatican II, colleges and universities recognized this reality and have tried to walk along with the students as they face new experiences. By definition, a Catholic institution offers a value system on various experiential and intellectual levels. Administrators and faculty members realize that they must integrate theory and practice: overemphasizing either theory or practice does not appropriately educate the talented young adults who study at Catholic institutions today. Many have concluded that they do the students a disservice if they pretend that all decisions are clear-cut and that ambiguity does not exist on many issues.

Roger Haight summarizes quite well the context of today's Church when he says that the challenge to being Christian is expressing one's beliefs in service or ministry. This is something that started with the community and developed into a structure "that in turn more clearly defined the historical form of the community." This ministry is pastoral when it serves the maintenance of the Church and missionary when it serves the mission of the Church. He adds: "These public forms of ministry can also be considered as representative of the kinds of active service that characterize the lives of all church members. Ministries organize the common spiritual activity of the whole community."[5]

Just as tensions have been felt historically between mission and maintenance in the Catholic Church, so also do emerging adults on Catholic college campuses struggle with a deep desire to serve, motivated by both social justice and their own developmental process into mature adulthood. The future of the Church depends on educated lay persons. The Church will not be credible or effective if it relies totally on structures that tend to be outdated. What better way to form new leaders for the Church than through a quality Catholic college education? That is precisely where campus ministry plays a very crucial role.

With the developments in higher education during the last half century, we note that just about every academic discipline has both theoretical and practical components. In the past, colleges and universities have frequently seen themselves as providing the theoretical aspects of a particular subject. They believed that the students would acquire the practical aspects on their own initiative. Today most instructors see that an integration of the two is necessary to give people a complete, well-rounded education in a given field, situated in a real-life context or career setting.

We contend that campus ministry at Catholic colleges is essential to the Catholic identity of these institutions of higher education. It provides the necessary reflection component to balance the classroom experience. Campus ministry helps guide people as they face the tensions that exist in trying to integrate their faith with the practice of that faith. The questions that students and faculty pose are based on real-life experience, not just on textbook content or classroom theory. At institutions where requirements in theology or religious studies are fairly minimal, these guided reflections and experiences from a faith perspective take on even more importance. When issues of funding arise, the administrators need to ask themselves: "How important is our Catholic identity? Are we willing to commit ourselves to make our campus ministry programs real vehicles to equip our students with the faith perspective they need to face the future with hope?"

Campus ministry serves several roles: It promotes the Catholic mission and identity at the institutional level. It bolsters and assists individuals on the personal level as they set about making major life decisions. Finally, it helps prepare the future leaders of the Church. As we have seen, over the last half century, campus ministry has emerged as an essential component of education at any institution of higher education that calls itself Catholic. As Catholic college and universities move forward in the twenty-first century, campus ministry is essential to the building up of a new, vibrant, and emergent Church.

RECOMMENDED READING

We recommend our 2009 book, *Being Catholic in a Changing World*, which examined problems and ambiguities in belief and practice that Catholics face in the contemporary world. It was also published by Paulist Press.

John O'Malley provides a very readable and historical overview of the Second Vatican Council in *What Happened at Vatican II* (Cambridge, MA: Belknap Press of Harvard University Press, 2008).

Raymond Brown shows the diversity in the early Church in his examination of seven early communities mentioned in the New Testament: Raymond E. Brown, *The Churches the Apostles Left Behind* (New York: Paulist Press, 1984).

NOTES

CHAPTER 1

1. *Gaudium et Spes* ("The Church in the Modern World"), no. 4 (New York: America Press, 1965), 102.

2. This whole statement can be found on the Web at http://archives.nd.edu/episodes/visitors/lol/idea.htm.

3. The National Catholic Educational Association uses the term *mission and vision* more often than *mission and identity*, and usually speaks of "Catholic identity." For the purposes of this book, these terms can be used interchangeably.

4. The January 2009 report of the Higher Education Research Institute of UCLA (HERI) highlights the growing diversity among all college students.

5. In 2003, UCLA's Higher Education Research Institute (HERI) studied the spirituality of college students. Concerning Catholics, HERI reported: "Students choosing Roman Catholic as their religious preference tend to score below the overall average on four measures: Religious Commitment, Religious Engagement, Religious/Social Conservatism, and Religious Skepticism. The Catholics' relatively low score on Skepticism is unusual, in the sense that students with low scores on the first three measures of religiousness ordinarily earn *high* scores on Religious Skepticism (e.g., Jewish students, Unitarians, Buddhists, and 'Nones')."

6. In their 2000 pastoral statement *Welcoming the Stranger among Us: Unity in Diversity*, the United States bishops emphasized

that the Church "embraces the rich cultural pluralism of this immigrant nation—what some call its 'multicultural' reality."

7. For instance, see Jai-Ok Kim, Sandra Forsythe, Qingliang Gu, Sook Jae Moon, "Cross-cultural Consumer Values, Needs and Purchase Behavior," in *Journal of Consumer Marketing* 19:6 (2002), 481–502.

8. http://www.monasticdialog.com/a.php?id=789, accessed March 31, 2011.

9. http://www.acommonword.com/index.php?lang=en&page=option1

10. In 1985 Pope John Paul II addressed 100,000 young Muslims in Casablanca on the religious and moral values common to Christianity and Islam. For his talk, see Gerald O'Collins, Daniel Kendall, and Jeffrey LaBelle, *Pope John Paul II: A Reader* (Mahwah, NJ: Paulist Press, 2007), 148–58.

11. This will be covered more extensively in chapter 2, which cites data from reports by CARA (Center of Applied Research in the Apostolate).

12. John Savard, "The Impact of Immersion Programs upon Undergraduate Students of Jesuit Colleges and Universities" (EdD dissertation, University of San Francisco, 2010). The institutions surveyed were Boston College, Canisius College, College of the Holy Cross, Fairfield University, Fordham University, Georgetown University, John Carroll University, LeMoyne College, Loyola University Maryland, Loyola University Chicago, Marquette University, Rockhurst College, Saint Louis University, Seattle University, Spring Hill College, University of Scranton, and the University of San Francisco. The countries where the immersion experiences took place were Belize, Dominican Republic, Ecuador, El Salvador, Ghana, Guatemala, Guyana, Honduras, India, Jamaica, Kenya, Mexico, Nicaragua, Peru, Poland, and Romania. In his comments to the authors of this book, Savard mentioned:

> It is obvious that comparatively few students are able to participate in international immersion programs, and assessment is needed to examine if their programs are get-

ting the bang for the buck. I believe that these programs do positively impact student participants. One of the issues regarding assessment is how a program influences a university culture. One of the things that I often think about is the "ripple" effect. If those who participate in immersion programs are student leaders, then assessment needs to take into account the impact that these leaders have upon the student body. That may not be insignificant.

Regarding the cost of international immersion programs, they are expensive to run, probably costing between $1,500 and $2,500 per student, including the cost of sending faculty and staff with the program, as well as all the costs associated with running any program. There is a possibility that assessment could show that immersions may be the most cost-effective programs available to enhance the mission at our [Jesuit] institutions.

13. This relationship is developed quite clearly in principle 6 of Sandra M. Estanek, Michael J. James, et al., *Principles for Good Practice for Student Affairs at Catholic Colleges and Universities* (Washington, DC: Association for Student Affairs at Catholic Colleges and Universities, 2007).

CHAPTER 2

1. National Catholic College Admissions Association (National CCAA) information retrieved on July 29, 2009, from http://www.catholiccollegesonline.org/.

2. Information regarding numbers of Catholic colleges and universities must be distinguished by the variety of institutions listed here, since not all of these have traditional undergraduate populations. Retrieved January 9, 2010, from http://www.accunet.org/i4a/pages/Index.cfm?pageID=3513#How_many_cath_coll.

3. National Center for Education Statistics (NCES).

4. Center for Applied Research in the Apostolate, *The Impact of Catholic Campus Ministry on the Beliefs and Worship Practices of U.S. Catholics* (Washington, DC: Georgetown University, 2005).

5. Center for Applied Research in the Apostolate, retrieved on February 26, 2011, from http://cara.georgetown.edu/AttendPR.pdf.

6. ACCU Web site, retrieved on January 9, 2010, from http://www.accunet.org/i4a/pages/Index.cfm?pageID=3513#How_many_cath_coll.

7. National CCAA's description of Catholic colleges and universities retrieved on January 9, 2010, from http://www.catholiccollegesonline.org/parents-students/top10.html.

8. Higher Education Research Institute, *The Spiritual Life of College Students* (Los Angeles: UCLA, 2004), 17.

9. Ibid., 4.

10. Ibid., 22.

11. *Princeton Review* information retrieved on February 26, 2011, from http://www.princetonreview.com/college/top-ten-majors.aspx. Also see the High School Graduate list of majors, accessed March 31, 2011, from http://www.thehighschoolgraduate.com/editorial/top-10-majors-for-2009.htm.

12. Donna Freitas, *Sex and the Soul: Juggling Sexuality, Spirituality, Romance, and Religion on America's College Campuses* (New York: Oxford University Press, 2008), 194.

13. Ibid., 200.

14. Ibid., 199.

15. Hart Research Associates, *Trends and Emerging Practices in General Education: Based on a Survey among Members of the Association of American Colleges and Universities* (Washington, DC: Hart Research Associates, 2009).

16. Higher Education Research Institute, *The American Freshman: National Norms for 2008* (Los Angeles: UCLA, 2009), 1.

17. Tim Muldoon, *Seeds of Hope: Young Adults and the Catholic Church in the United States* (Mahwah, NJ: Paulist Press, 2008), 146.

18. Ibid., 145–46.
19. Ibid., 163.
20. Higher Education Research Institute, *The Spiritual Life of College Students*, 22.

CHAPTER 3

1. *Gaudium et Spes* ("The Church in the Modern World"), no. 1, in *The Documents of Vatican II* (New York: America Press, 1966), 199–200.

2. According to the National Institute of Mental Health (NIMH), "In 2006, suicide was the third leading cause of death for young people ages 15 to 24. Of every 100,000 young people in each age group, the following number died by suicide: Children ages 10 to 14—1.3 per 100,000; Adolescents ages 15 to 19—8.2 per 100,000; Young adults ages 20 to 24—12.5 per 100,000." Retrieved from http://www.nimh. nih.gov/health/publications/suicide-in-the-us-statistics-and-prevention/ index.shtml#children.

3. The Campus Ministry Leadership Institute at St. Joseph University and the Frank J. Lewis Institute for Campus Ministry Orientation are two excellent examples of these opportunities. Information on their summer training institutes can be found at their respective Web sites: http:// www.sju.edu/cmli/ and http://www.nccbuscc.org/education/highered/ lewisbrochure.shtml.

4. Adolph Guggenbuhl-Craig, *Power in the Helping Professions* (New York: Spring Publications, 2009).

5. More information about clinical pastoral education programs can be found at the National Association of Catholic Chaplains Web site at http://www.nacc.org/certification/cpeCenters.asp, or directly from the Association for Clinical Pastoral Education, Inc., Web site at http://www. acpe.edu/DirectoriesRegions.html.

6. Formal certification is provided by the Catholic Campus Ministry Association, whose standards and procedures are approved by the United States Conference of Catholic Bishops Commission on Certification and

Accreditation (USCCB/CCA). Such certification is a distinction for a campus minister, signifying a high level of competence, as well as significant personal, theological, and spiritual reflection. Certification is valid for seven years.

7. Jeffrey LaBelle, SJ, and Daniel Kendall, SJ, *Being Catholic in a Changing World* (Mahwah, NJ: Paulist Press, 2009).

8. Tim Muldoon, *Seeds of Hope: Young Adults and the Catholic Church in the United States* (Mahwah, NJ: Paulist Press, 2008), 162.

9. More information about this organization can be found at the following Web site: http://www.ccmanet.org/ccma.nsf/index?OpenForm.

CHAPTER 4

1. "Depth, Universality, and Learned Ministry: Challenges to Jesuit Higher Education Today" (Networking Jesuit Higher Education: Shaping the Future for a Humane, Just, Sustainable Globe, Mexico City, April 23, 2010). Father Nicolás's address can be found at www.uia.mx/shapingthefuture/files/NicolasSJ-JHE-April232010.pdf, page 10. The quotation from Pope Benedict XVI refers to *Caritas in Veritate*, no. 56.

2. Nicolás, 9.

3. Ibid., 6.

4. "Statement on the Nature of the Contemporary Catholic University," http://archives.nd.edu/episodes/visitors/lol/idea.htm, no. 9.

CHAPTER 5

1. "What Are the Characteristics of Service-Learning?" Posted on the National Service-Learning Clearinghouse Web site and taken mostly from Eyler and Giles. The description was retrieved on January 28, 2010, from http://www.servicelearning.org/what_is_service-learning/characteristics.

2. Janet Eyler and Dwight E. Giles, Jr., *Where's the Learning in Service-Learning?* (San Francisco: Jossey-Bass Publishers, 1999), xi.

3. Ibid, 8.

4. Andrew Furco, "Service-Learning: A Balanced Approach to Experiential Education," in *Expanding Boundaries: Service and Learning*, ed. Barbara Taylor (Washington, DC: Corporation for National Service, 1996), 6.

5. Hart Research Associates, *Trends and Emerging Practices in General Education* (Washington, DC: Association of American Colleges and Universities, May 2009), 8.

6. Nicholas R. Santilli, "Don't Call Us Millennials!" *Conversations*, no. 37 (Spring 2010), 11.

7. Sandra M. Estanek, Michael J. James, et al., *Principles for Good Practice for Student Affairs at Catholic Colleges and Universities* (Washington, DC: Association for Student Affairs at Catholic Colleges and Universities, 2007), nos. 3 and 4.

8. *College Students Helping America* (Washington, DC: Corporation for National and Community Service, 2006), page 2. The full booklet was retrieved on January 28, 2010, from http://www.nationalservice.gov/pdf/06_1016_RPD_college_full.pdf.

9. Ibid.

10. Robert Bellah, et. al, *Habits of the Heart: Individualism and Commitment in American Life* (Berkeley, CA: University of California Press, 1996).

11. Ira Shor, "Can Critical Teaching Foster Activism in This Time of Repression?" *Radical Teacher* 79, no. 39 (Fall 2007), 129.

CHAPTER 6

1. These comments were taken from Robert Frank with Tom Meltzer, et al., *The Best 371 Colleges: 2010 Edition* (New York: The Princeton Review, Inc., 2009), 692. The particular institution referred to is the University of San Francisco.

2. Ibid.

3. Ibid.

4. Raymond Brown, *An Introduction to the New Testament*, The Anchor Bible Reference Library (New York: Doubleday, 1996), 511; parenthesis in the original.

5. A good reference book on this subject is Gerald O'Collins, *Salvation for All: God's Other Peoples* (Oxford: Oxford University Press, 2008).

6. "Address to Young Muslims in Morocco, August 19, 1985," in Gerald O'Collins, Daniel Kendall, and Jeffrey LaBelle, *Pope John Paul II: A Reader* (Mahwah, NJ: Paulist Press, 2007), 148–58.

7. *Notre Dame Observer* (February 19, 2008), found at http://media.www.ndsmcobserver.com/media/storage/paper660/news/2008/02/19/Viewpoint/Engage.In.The.Churchs.Thinking-3218043.shtml.

CHAPTER 7

1. "Men [and Women] for Others: Education for Social Justice and Social Action Today" (address, Tenth International Congress of Jesuit Alumni of Europe, Valencia, July 31, 1973). Retrieved on February 18, 2010, from http://onlineministries.creighton.edu/CollaborativeMinistry/men-for-others.html.

2. *Circular Letter 36*. Retrieved on February 23, 2010, from http://www.up.edu/holycross/.

3. Retrieved on February 23, 2010, from http://www.marianist.com/ministries.php?pid=83.

4. For more information on vocations, see http://www.vocation.com/, especially http://www.vocations.com/discern/index.htm regarding discernment.

5. *Gaudium et Spes* ("The Church in the Modern World"), nos. 1, 2, in *The Documents of Vatican II* (New York: America Press, 1966), 199–200.

6. Ibid., no. 43, page 243.

7. "Abington School District v. Schempp," cited in Robert Alley, *The Constitution and Religion: Leading Supreme Court Cases on Church and State* (Amherst, NY: Prometheus Books, 1999), 188.

8. General Congregation 32, "Decree 4: The Service of Faith and the Promotion of Justice," in *Jesuit Life & Mission Today*, ed. John W. Padberg, SJ (St. Louis: Institute of Jesuit Sources, 2009), 305.

9. John Donne, "Meditation XVII," in *The Complete Poetry and Selected Prose of John Donne & The Complete Poetry of William Blake*, ed. Geoffrey Keynes (New York: Random House, 1941), 331–32.

CHAPTER 8

1. Pope John XXIII, *Gaudet Mater Ecclesia* ("Mother Church Rejoices"), in *The Documents of Vatican II* (New York: America Press, 1966), 712–13.

2. Jon Sobrino, *The True Church and the Poor* (Maryknoll, NY: Orbis, 1984), 265; the quotation is from a chapter of particular interest, "Evangelization as Mission of the Church."

3. Jürgen Moltmann, *The Church in the Power of the Spirit: A Contribution to Messianic Ecclesiology* (London: SCM Press, 1977), 10. We are indebted to Roger Haight's analysis, "Expanding the Exercises," which appears in *Studies in the Spirituality of Jesuits* 42:2 (Summer 2010): 26–28.

4. Available at http://bartleby.net/124/pres56.html.

5. Haight, "Expanding the Exercises," 36–37.